bright
toddler

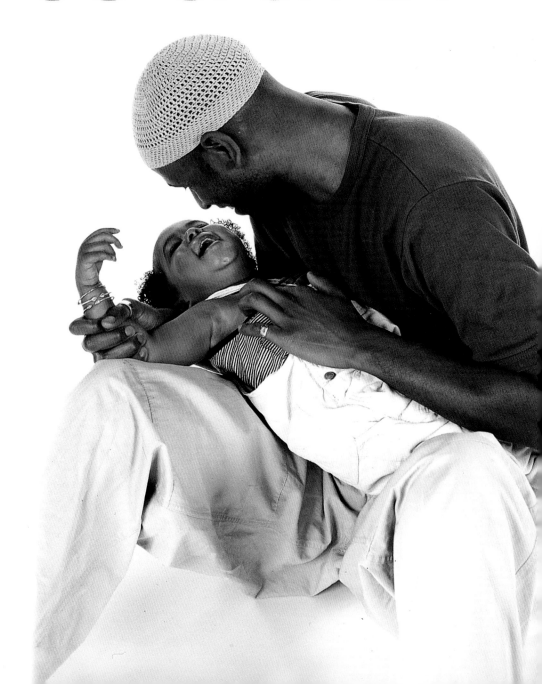

bright
toddler

Dr Richard C. Woolfson

hamlyn

Contents

Language   84

Learning   102

Social and Emotional Development   120

The Importance of Stimulation

Between 15 months and 3 years, your toddler develops at an amazing rate, and his curiosity and thirst for knowledge seem insatiable. He becomes more physically agile and he grows more sociable. At the beginning of his second year he prefers to watch other children from a distance. Within a few months he will probably enjoy playing alongside others of his own age, and by the end of his third year he starts to mix with them. This phase of your toddler's life sees a surge in his independence, with temporary peaks and troughs in his self-confidence. You can help his development by providing appropriate stimulation that encourages him to discover himself and the world around him so that he becomes a bright toddler.

A Journey of Discovery

Your growing toddler has an innate desire to explore uncharted territory, and he does everything he can to learn new things all the time. This determination to understand his surroundings, to interact with other children, and to have more control over himself and his environment continues throughout his second and third years.

Curiosity is a major stimulant to his learning. For instance, your toddler's determination to see what lies at the top, motivates him to climb up stairs – even though negotiating the steps remains a big physical challenge for him. But that's not the only reason that he wants to ascend the entire flight of stairs. The fact is that he needs to prove to himself that he can do it; the beaming smile that breaks across his face as he finally clambers up the last step is all the evidence you need that he is proud of his own achievements.

You'll find that your toddler is always on the go, ready to explore at every opportunity. A lot of the time he provides his own amusement by investigating anything that is near him and that attracts his curiosity. For example, when left alone in the sitting room your 18-month-old will perhaps

Above: This little girl's expression of delight shows her pleasure at having reached the top step by herself.

delve into the cupboards and empty their contents onto the floor. At the age of 2 years, he'll be prepared to have a go on the climbing frame in the garden or park, just to see what it's like. And by the time he's 3 years old, he'll be learning new physical and social skills from playing with children his own age.

Left: A toddler's instinct is to explore her environment physically and she will love the challenge of climbing stairs.

You'll be delighted when you see your toddler making these new discoveries. It's almost as though he's learning without any help from you at all, and to some extent that's true. But the knowledge and new skills he acquires between the ages of 15 months and 3 years, learned through his own efforts, are based on the stimulation you provide.

✦✦✦✦ Top ✦ Tips ✦✦✦✦

1. Don't dominate. The challenge facing you as his parent is to provide a high level of stimulation without taking over from him completely. Remember that the two of you are working together to promote his development.

2. Enjoy playing with him. If you don't enjoy playing with him and if he doesn't enjoy being with you, his rate of learning will slow down. So look on the activities you provide as fun, not learning, and make sure there is plenty of laughter every day.

3. Give your toddler space. You don't need to hover over him all the time in an attempt to ensure that he learns at every opportunity. He loves stimulation from you, but he also enjoys having room to explore and learn on his own.

4. Give appropriate activities. Strike a balance between encouraging him to progress and pushing him so hard that he gives up altogether. Tune in to his level of understanding and abilities and then give him a suitable activity.

5. Delight in his achievements. Whatever his talents and abilities, your toddler is a very special child. He's wonderful and he needs you to tell him this. Show your pleasure at every new skill he acquires.

Progressing in Partnership

Using the suggestions in this book enables you to enhance and enrich your child's everyday experiences. Look on it as a partnership between you and your toddler, that merges his innate talents and drive with your plan of action. This will create a dynamic interaction, resulting in an interesting and challenging life for him.

But it's not just about promoting his learning: there are emotional benefits, too. After all, every toddler thrives on love and attention from a parent. He adores your interest and probably tries that little bit harder when he knows you are watching. You'll catch him glancing up at you, proud of his own achievements, hoping to see a similar expression on your face. And if he does, then he keeps going.

You benefit as well. Interacting with your toddler in a positive way – not just when he misbehaves or needs to be fed – enhances your relationship with him. The emotional connection between the two of you strengthens as a result of working together, because each of you gets to know the other in new ways. He learns that you can be a source of fun and support, and you learn about his abilities. This increased closeness builds his confidence – your child will be ready to try new challenges in this frame of mind.

Below: A close and loving relationship with your child is vital in giving her the confidence to learn and develop.

Using this Book

The more you understand the nature of your child's development from 15 months to 3 years the better placed you'll be to promote her progress. This book helps you along this road of understanding by identifying the key areas of psychological development that your toddler experiences during this fascinating period in her life. But try to take a broad view, rather than considering each area of development in isolation, because all of these different aspects of your toddler's growth interact. This book advocates an all-round approach to stimulating your toddler as this balanced way of promoting your child's development is more effective than concentrating on one feature alone.

How to Use this Book

There are many ways in which we can categorize aspects of infant development. This book focuses on five main dimensions:

• **movement.** This is your child's ability to move her arms, legs and body in a coordinated and purposeful way. At 15 months, she can walk independently and go wherever she wants, even up and down stairs. By 3 years, she can balance on her tiptoes, she can jump off a step without toppling over when she lands, and she can even stand on one foot while the other is raised from the ground and make her first attempts at hopping.

• **hand–eye coordination.** During her second year she begins to make marks on a piece of paper while holding a crayon, and by the end of her third year her hand control is likely to have improved to such an extent that she can copy a circle that you draw on the paper for her. She may try to catch a ball rolled along the ground towards her. She also enjoys helping you tidy toys

away, and will copy your actions, such as dusting the table.

• **language.** You've already heard her first word by the time she reaches 15 months – and probably several more too! Her speech and language continue to develop rapidly, so that by her third birthday she probably uses well over a thousand words in her everyday speech (including pronouns), and she also begins to understand grammatical rules.

• **learning.** The thirst for learning that was so apparent in your child's first 15 months continues unabated through the toddler stage. At the start of this period of her development, her memory is just good enough to recall where she placed her last toy. By the time she reaches her third birthday she is transformed into a child who can accurately compare two different quantities and who can tell you about some special event that she experienced days ago.

• **social and emotional.** Your child continues to have a close emotional

Above: At around 3 years your toddler will have mastered a huge range of physical skills including running and jumping.

attachment to you throughout her second and third years, and this gives her the emotional stability to form social relationships with other children. She may not play cooperatively with children by the time she's 3 years old but she loves their company.

Be Flexible

You may have a plan for your toddler's development, but you can be sure she has a different one! In other words, every toddler is a unique individual. That's why you should look on this book as a guide only, not as a fixed programme of activities and exercises.

The same applies to the different areas of development described in this book. Although, for example, language development is outlined in a different chapter from hand–eye coordination, and although learning is described separately from emotional and social development, each area of development interacts with the others. When your toddler finally manages to climb the stairs on her own – a physical achievement – this boosts her confidence, which makes her more eager to try more challenges – an emotional advance. Likewise, her improved understanding of language means that she is able to follow directions more effectively, enabling her to learn from your advice.

So there is no fixed way of using this book. Just remember that your child needs stimulation in all areas and that whatever constructive activities you undertake together will benefit her as long as you have a relaxed approach.

Below: Learning at this age doesn't have to be planned or structured – the garden and park, for example, provide a wealth of stimulating experiences.

❖❖❖❖ Top ❖ Tips ❖❖❖❖

1. Establish an overview. Make a point of dipping in and out of all the chapters regularly, to help you maintain a general overview of your toddler's development. You'll help her more effectively if you keep a broad view.

2. Trial and error. Your toddler's individual personality means that she will enjoy some of the activities, and dislike others. That's fine – no single activity is vital for her development. So don't get into a confrontation with her – just go on to something else.

3. Don't get stuck on ages. Remind yourself that the ages given in this book are only guidelines. You'll no doubt find that your toddler does some things earlier than suggested and some things later. This is perfectly normal.

4. Use your imagination. Don't be afraid to make up activities of your own if an idea occurs to you. Use different toys from the ones suggested, if you think they would best suit your own child.

5. Avoid pushing her too hard. The activities given in this book are not tests that she must pass at a particular time. When she can't manage a particular activity or game, come back to it in a few weeks when she is ready or skip it altogether.

6. Have fun. Toddlers are a delight to be with. Use this book to enhance your enjoyment of your child at this stage, but don't let it rule your time together.

Your Attitude

You need to take a balanced, positive attitude when it comes to stimulating your toddler. And that means making sure that you do neither too much with him nor too little. If he is under-stimulated, you may notice that he becomes bored or perhaps listless; and if he is over-stimulated, he could become miserable, tired and irritable with everything. Of course, it's not easy to get the balance right, but as you involve him in the activities suggested throughout this book keep a close watch on his reactions. Monitor his responses carefully to avoid either extreme.

Getting the Balance Right

The best way to determine whether or not you are achieving a suitable level of stimulation is to note any significant mood changes. Typical signs of under-stimulation include a general level of passivity in which he shows little interest in his toys, lack of animation in his body language and facial expression, and a higher than usual level of tiredness. You may also find that he is unusually quiet and becomes easily upset over things that he usually takes in his stride.

Right: If your toddler feels pressurized she may lose interest, but if you let her have some time to herself her motivation will soon reappear.

Typical signs of over-stimulation include a high level of activity because he feels the need to be on the go the whole time, a disrupted sleep pattern, and fluctuating and unpredictable levels of concentration. Be on the lookout for these warning signs to ensure you get the balance right. In most instances, however, there is a greater danger of over-stimulation than under-stimulation. There are a number of reasons for this.

First, you have a natural desire to encourage your toddler to

achieve his highest potential and this may drive you unwittingly towards providing him with a higher level of stimulation than he actually needs. Secondly, you may believe that stimulation, no matter how much, can only benefit your child because there is always more to learn. Of course his capacity to absorb new information is never used up, but stimulation has to be paced appropriately for your child or his motivation will soon ebb away. Thirdly, you probably

compare him to other toddlers of his own age, matching his rate of development against theirs. Any indication that he is less advanced than other children of his age (and there's always someone more advanced than your child) may make you feel under pressure to push him more.

1. Be honest with yourself. You're only human; there will be plenty of times when playing with your child is the last thing you feel like doing. If you reach this stage, just stop and rest. Stimulating activities work best when you are both in the mood for them.

2. Avoid too much structure. Free time is important for your toddler. It allows him the space to make choices for himself. If you plan every activity for him, he could soon lose the confidence to keep himself amused when you don't organize his play for him.

3. Enjoy his successes. Stimulation has to be fun or it will become too clinical. If you rush from one activity to the next as if ticking off a checklist, you'll find it hard to savour the pleasure from your toddler's achievements.

4. Let him play with other children. When he is with others his own age, he'll find the level of stimulation that suits him best and spontaneously pace himself according to the demands of the situation.

5. Relax. Development is not a race. There is no real advantage in your toddler being able to complete challenges normally associated with an older child. Aim for his progress to be at his own steady pace.

Do your best to resist these pressures towards over-stimulation. As long as you are aware of the risk and occasionally step back and think about what you are doing with your toddler, the chances of over-stimulating him remain low.

There's no ideal amount of time you should spend on the activities in this book. Much depends on your and your toddler's inclinations, your family routine, and his level of development. Also remember that he is receiving stimulation for much of the time anyway, just by watching what goes on around him and by being involved in daily activities around the home, such as washing, dressing, feeding, going to the toilet, and so on.

The best arrangement is to integrate the suggested activities into his normal play pattern so that they appear natural rather than contrived. As a rough guide, in most instances spend only around five minutes at a time on any one activity – if he's still struggling to

Right: A happy and animated child who is absorbed in her activities is the best indication that you are providing the right level of stimulation.

achieve the target after that, it's time to give him and you a break. Certainly, there is absolutely no point in continuing once his interest and attention has faded. You can't force a 2-year-old to be enthusiastic; he needs gentle encouragement, not pressure.

When you have decided that both you and your toddler have had enough of an activity, move on to something new, such as taking a walk or letting him choose what toy he wants to play with. You'll probably find that this recharges his enthusiasm, making him ready to learn once again. Don't get annoyed with him when he doesn't learn at the speed you hope for – he's doing his best, and your irritation will tend to put him off the activity in the future.

Summary of

Development

Nature or Nurture

Most psychologists accept that a toddler's development is partly influenced by the abilities she is born with and partly by the way she is raised at home. Of course, it's difficult to know the relative significance of each of these factors. Your own views affect the way you interact with and stimulate your toddler. A parent who is convinced that innate talent is more important than acquired skills in determining a child's development may prefer to take a back-seat role, convinced that their child will achieve her potential without much intervention. On the other hand, a parent who believes in the primary role of the environment in determining development will be more likely to take a pro-active approach to providing structured activities.

The Debate

Here are some of the arguments given in favour of the 'nature' argument (that is, the view that development during the pre-school years is primarily determined by inherited characteristics):

• **there is no doubt that children inherit some physical features from their parents** – for example, the colour of hair and eyes. This shows that some characteristics are certainly inherited and it is logical to assume that other tendencies are also passed on genetically.

• **scientific investigation into genetic structures has found that the blueprint for many aspects of development is already laid down at conception.** For instance, your toddler's genes determine the maximum height that she will reach, her optimum body weight and when she'll start to grow hair.

• **studies have shown that parents with a strong musical ability generally have children who have above average capacity to learn a musical instrument.** This musical inclination shows through without any prompting at all and does not stem from intense stimulation by the parents.

• **there are occasional instances of child prodigies,** in other words, extremely gifted children whose talent shows through even though their parents don't exhibit the same exceptional skills. This is taken as additional proof that such characteristics are inborn.

Right: A child's individuality arises from the interaction between her inherited characteristics and her environment, making her different in talent and temperament from her siblings.

Here are some of the arguments in favour of the 'nurture' argument (the view that development during the pre-school years is mainly governed by the level of stimulation that is provided at home):

• **parents who are well educated themselves usually place a high value on early stimulation** and therefore provide a full programme of activities for their toddler. As a result of this input, their child tends to develop at a faster rate – and this is one reason why parents and children tend to have similar levels of achievement.

• **investigations have demonstrated that parental behaviour greatly affects child development.** For instance, numerous research projects have shown that parents tend to accept aggressive behaviour from boys but discourage such behaviour in girls. This could be why boys generally show more aggression than girls.

• **common sense and everyday experience tells you that what you do affects your child.** Think of any song you have taught your toddler. She couldn't have learned this by herself; she needed you to teach her the words and tune. You can probably think of lots of similar learning experiences.

• **there have been numerous long-term projects that have successfully boosted the development of pre-school children through a planned programme of activities.** If everything is entirely due to nature and has nothing to do with nurture, this sort of intervention would be completely ineffective.

A Bit of Both

Both sides in this debate are able to present convincing arguments, but neither extreme point of view is, however, likely to be correct. For most of us it is clear that the way a toddler develops is a mixture of her innate abilities that were present at birth and her upbringing. It's the delicate interaction between both of these influences that counts.

The practical lessons for parents that arise out of this debate are: don't leave it all to chance in the hope that your toddler's natural talents will shine through; and don't have unrealistically high expectations of her in the belief that she can achieve anything as long as she receives the right sort of stimulation. Your input is most effective when it is carefully measured and closely matches your toddler's own individual pattern of development.

Below: Tailor your parental input to each child's personality and aptitude; even within the same family children often develop different skills at very different rates.

✦✦✦ Top·Tips ✦✦✦

1. Get involved anyway. You have already discovered that playing with your toddler has more impact than ignoring her. Her emotional reaction tells you that she prefers to have your attention than to be ignored.

2. Expect progress in small stages. Your toddler is unlikely to make large gains overnight in any area of development. Progress is usually slow and steady, so instead watch for small steps forward.

3. Identify her interests. Find out the activities, toys and games that usually grab her attention and use these as the starting point for further stimulating activities. Introduce new ones periodically in order to broaden her interests.

4. Persist even if progress is slow. The fact that your child makes slow progress in one area does not mean she'll always be a slow learner. She has the potential to progress and it's up to you to keep encouraging her until she moves to the next stage.

5. Accept her individuality. She's not the same as her brother, or her sister, or your friend's child – she is a unique individual who will develop during the early years at her own pace. She needs you to love her for who she actually is and her own special achievements.

Sibling Rivalry

A two-year age gap between children is common, so when your first child is around the age of 2, your second child may be due or even have arrived. However, the moment you have your second child – in fact, the moment your first-born realizes he has a little brother or sister on the way – you need to consider the possibility of sibling rivalry. Jealousy between children in the same family is so common that most psychologists regard it as normal, and it arises because your children compete for a share of your time and attention. However, there is lots you can do to ease sibling rivalry.

About Sibling Rivalry

Your toddler may show jealousy of brothers and sisters in a variety of ways. For example, a 2-year-old may become moody around the time the new baby arrives; or a 3-year-old might complain that his little brother constantly plays with his toys without asking. But sibling rivalry isn't just confined to the first-born child. There is research evidence that second and third children can resent a new baby, even though they are already used to living with others in the family. And younger children can be jealous of older siblings, which is why your 18-month-old toddler might burst into tears when he sees you cuddling his older sister; he wants all your love for himself.

If your child is around the age of 2 when your second child is born, he will probably express his jealousy by hitting his sibling rather than by complaining to you. Fortunately this pattern changes as he gets older, making such physical expressions of jealousy less likely.

Left: Encourage your toddler to talk to and play with a new baby but make sure you give him one-to-one attention as well.

Above: It will help a toddler to accept a new baby if you spend time before the birth explaining what is going to happen.

The age gap between your children can also have an effect on the intensity of jealousy between them. Sibling rivalry tends to be greatest when the age gap between children is between 18 months and 2 years, and it tends to be lowest when the age gap is either much smaller or much larger than this. If your first-born is very young at the time of the birth of your second baby, he will barely notice the new arrival because he is so concerned with himself; and if your first-born is several years older he is less likely to feel threatened by the presence of a new baby because he is more secure in his relationships and he has an established daily routine.

When He's Just a Toddler

It's the in-between age gap that causes most problems. The typical toddler likes to have everything his own way and he expects the world to revolve around him. From this perspective, it is understandable that he may be upset by the arrival of a new baby in the family, because that younger sibling needs plenty of attention, too.

If you are expecting your second child while your first-born is still a young toddler, tell him about the new baby once the pregnancy starts to show, probably around the fourth or fifth month. Explain that you'll still love him just as much as ever and that the new baby will love him, too. He needs your reassurance at this time, so answer any questions he has openly and honestly. Involve him in the pregnancy and let him feel the baby move in the tummy so that he can feel part of this very

important family event. Let him buy a present for the new baby and make sure that the new baby has a present for him at their first meeting (if you are having your baby in hospital, pack this in your bag before you go in).

Remember that your first child just needs to feel loved and valued, especially when the new baby is the focus of attention. Despite the hectic routine of caring for a newborn at the same time as looking after a toddler, try to make some special time for your first-born on his own every day to remind him that you love him as much as ever.

Below: Although sibling rivalry will crop up from time to time, it often eases once your children can share activities and games with each other.

Gender Differences

There are well-documented developmental differences between boys and girls, both physical and psychological. For instance, girls tend to pass through the major developmental stages earlier than boys, including walking, talking, potty training and self-help skills. In addition, girls tend to have better concentration, are better at listening to instructions, are less likely to develop fussy eating habits and usually learn to read and count at an earlier age. The challenge facing you is to encourage your child to develop as an individual, irrespective of gender – and the best way to achieve this is through awareness of potential gender-related influences.

Facts about Gender

Here are some other facts about gender differences between the age of 15 months and 3 years:

• **boys tend to be more adventurous than girls;** they are more likely to take risks. But this slight tendency may be reinforced by parents who tacitly accept this type of behaviour from boys but discourage it from girls.

• **girls are quicker at learning how to cooperate with each other.** By the age of 3 years, they are able to play games quietly together, while boys of the same age are more likely to bicker with each other in that situation.

• **parents tend to react differently to boys and girls.** For example, they are more likely to tolerate aggressive behaviour from a boy than from a girl – in most families, aggression is discouraged immediately when shown by a girl.

Your child's awareness of gender differences is firmly established by the age of 15 months. By then, she

is consistently able to tell whether a 1-year-old is a boy or a girl – even when that 1-year-old wears non-gender specific (unisex) clothing. For instance, if your girl of this age mixes with children wearing unisex clothing she will tend to stay beside the girls (and a boy will tend to stay beside the boys), despite the fact that she probably couldn't say why she does this.

Over the next six months or so, you'll begin to see a pattern of gender preferences for toys emerge, though this may be influenced by you and your values. Two-year-olds generally like to play with toys associated with their gender (for example, most boys like toy cars and rough-and-tumble play, while most girls prefer dolls and imaginative play). And by the end of the third year, your child's view of gender usually follows the sex-stereotypes that are found in society as a whole. This adds further weight to the social theory of gender development. For instance, most

Above: Girls often seem more careful than boys although this may be due to the fact that parents unconsciously tend to discourage girls from taking risks.

3-year-olds (boys and girls) think girls are better at cooking and cleaning and that boys are better at construction activities.

The Source of Gender

One explanation of gender differences is based on the scientific fact that there are obviously biological differences between boys and girls. For example, during pregnancy and at birth, boys have a higher level of the male sex hormone testosterone in their bodies, which is linked to aggression and high activity. And there are those who claim that since women are physically equipped to bear children, they must have a

Above: A boy's apparently fearless behaviour may stem from the fact that his parents tacitly encourage this attitude.

biological instinct to be caring and domesticated. These arguments are used to explain why girls enjoy playing with dolls while boys often prefer more adventurous activities.

The other main explanation of gender differences rests on the assumption that these differences are learned – for example, in the different types of toys that are often bought for boys (cars, construction kits) and girls (dolls, toy kitchens), and also by the language used to praise children of each sex – brave or strong for boys, pretty or kind for girls. Through this process, these theorists claim, gender differences are reinforced by the views on gender differences that parents already hold.

There is no clear answer to this debate on the origins of gender differences. It stands to reason that there is a biological component to gender differences but it also makes sense to accept that the influence of parents must also play a part. These separate factors interact powerfully to create your child's overall views on gender.

❖❖❖❖ Top ❖ Tips ❖❖❖❖

1. Be self-aware. Think about your own attitudes to boys and girls. For instance, be prepared to give as much encouragement to your girl when she shows signs of being adventurous as you would to your boy in the same situation.

2. Give your toddler access to a wide range of toys. Let her choose which toys she wants to play with. Don't worry if your 2-year-old girl shows interest in toys you normally associate with boys or vice versa.

3. Show affection to your child, whether a boy or girl. Your boy likes to be loved and cuddled by you just as much as a girl. No matter what his individual personality traits, he wants your attention, love and plenty of hugs.

4. Have confidence in your parenting ability. Rely on your instincts, and don't be concerned over what others tell you about the way boys should behave and the way girls should behave. There is no 'should' about it – it really is entirely up to you.

5. Set a good example. Your child's views on gender are influenced by your attitudes. If she sees, for instance, that only women make her meals and play with her, she'll grow up thinking this is the sole province of women.

Childcare Arrangements

For many parents, the toddler phase signals their own return to work (either full-time or part-time); it is often selected as the time to resume a career that was temporarily suspended while tackling parenthood on a full-time basis. This return to employment is a huge step for both you and your child, and means you have to make satisfactory arrangements for childcare. You need to think carefully about the options available, whether a nanny, childminder, crèche or nursery. Whatever care arrangement you make, be sure that it is one that suits you and your child and that it is of a high quality – if not, you will both lose out.

The Right Option

Some parents are lucky enough to have a trusted relative who lives close enough to look after their young child while they are out at work. In cases when this is not possible, the most popular childcare options for toddlers are nannies, who look after the child in the home, or childminders, who look after one or more extra children in their own home, perhaps alongside their own children. There are also various types of nurseries and crèches, in which several carers look after children in a separate premises, but not all of these cater for under-3s on a full-time basis.

When selecting someone to care for your child while you work – whether you leave the child at the carer's place of work or the carer comes to your house – there are specific criteria to consider:

• **qualifications in childcare and education.** Qualifications on their own are no guarantee of quality of care, but they at least demonstrate the carer's seriousness about their job, their knowledge of child development and education, and their ability to think about issues concerning the management of young children.

• **previous experience in childcare and education.** As with qualifications, previous experience on its own doesn't guarantee quality. However, you will probably be more comfortable knowing that your child is under the supervision of someone who is well used to dealing with children that age.

• **references from other parents.** Be wary of leaving your child with someone who is unable to supply a reference from another parent. A written testimonial could be acceptable, but better still is the opportunity to talk to at least a couple of parents who have previously used this carer for their own children.

Left: When selecting childcare, talk to other parents who have resumed work to help you weigh up the various options.

• **registration.** Where there is a statutory requirement for a carer to conform to the standards of a registration scheme that inspects levels of suitability and safety, check that the carer you are considering is fully registered. This does not by itself guarantee quality of care, but it should ensure a minimum level.

✦✦✦✦ Top · Tips ✦✦✦✦

1. Be positive about the situation. Remind yourself that the variety of activities that your child receives from a competent and sensitive carer will add a further dimension to the quality of his life. He can benefit from this extra stimulation.

2. Explain about the carer beforehand. A week before he is due to start with his carer, tell your child about the arrangements you have made. Be ready to answer any questions he might have, and adopt an upbeat attitude about it.

3. Make a visit. A few days before your child is due to start with the carer, arrange for the two of them to meet. This lets your child grow accustomed to the idea. Meeting his carer in advance reassures and excites him.

4. Show interest in his activities. Once your child has returned to your care each day, talk to him about his activities with the carer. Let him see that you are deeply interested in what he does while he is not with you.

5. Talk regularly with the carer. It's important that you have a regular report of your child's progress from the carer. That way you can make sure that any minor difficulties are resolved before they turn into major problems.

The difficulties facing you are, first, that you may be under pressure to make a quick decision because a job is waiting for you, and second, that the carers you initially approach may have a full commitment already. Yet you should do your best to avoid acting impulsively or cutting corners in order to reach a speedy decision. Your child is a very precious part of your life and he deserves the best care possible while you are elsewhere. Check out the options carefully and thoroughly before deciding on the answer.

Making Up your Mind

Having considered the above factors and having met the potential carer, ask yourself these questions:

• **am I at ease with this carer?** The fact is that if you don't feel at ease in the company of the carer, then it is unlikely that your child will feel any easier. Follow your instinctive reaction to the person.

• **if I was a child, would I want to spend time in the company of this person?** Try to look at it from your child's point of view, and imagine what it would be like for him to spend regular amounts of time with this person.

• **do the carer's views on child development coincide with mine?** Remember that you are the child's parent at all times. It stands to reason that you'll want a carer who thinks the same way you do about ways to stimulate children, and about matters such as food choices, safety and discipline.

• **what will the carer offer my child?** Every effective carer should have a clear idea about the kinds of stimulating activities they intend to

Above: Talk to your child about what he has done while you have been at work – he will enjoy telling you about his day.

provide for the children in their care, and should be able to outline this easily to you.

• **how does the carer link with parents?** You need to keep in touch with what happens during your child's time with the carer. Make sure that you will be able to find regular opportunities to talk about your child's progress and to consult about any problems.

• **what kind of social life will the carer provide?** Your child needs to have a healthy social life with plenty of opportunities for mixing with other children his own age. Ask how the carer will provide this and, if working from their own home, ascertain whether their family situation is suitable for your child.

Once you are satisfied on all these points – and assuming the hours, location and cost suit you – make the commitment. By approaching the selection meticulously you can return to work knowing that your child is in good hands.

Non-Verbal Communication

Although your toddler's spoken language develops considerably during this second and third year – and this gradually becomes her preferred means of communication – she also continues to use body language in order to express her feelings and ideas to you. Both forms of communication run side by side. For instance, your child conveys her feelings through facial expression, breathing rate, body posture, and arm and leg movements. The more you can understand her body language at this stage, the closer the emotional connection between you and your child will become. As well as tuning into her non-verbal communication, there is lots you can do to encourage her to use it more effectively.

Dimensions of your Toddler's Non-Verbal Communication

The main features of body language between the ages of 15 months and 3 years are:

• **crying.** This remains your child's most natural way of letting you know that she is unhappy. She doesn't need to say a word – her tears of distress tell you that she's miserable or annoyed or angry.

• **facial expression.** She can convey a whole range of emotions simply by changing the expression on her face. Just by looking at her appearance, you can tell when she is, for instance, happy, sad, afraid, uncomfortable, in pain or angry.

• **arm and hand movements.** When she's relaxed and contented, her hands will probably lie open by her side, fingers spread out. However, clenched fists, for instance, silently tell you that she's tense or raging about something.

• **leg and feet movements.** Now that she is fully mobile, she can simply walk away from a situation she dislikes. Swinging her legs while sitting in a chair could mean that she's having a good time or that she's bored.

• **posture.** When your toddler stands or sits with slumped shoulders and head hanging down, she is probably troubled, even

though she hasn't said a word to you about whatever is worrying her. But shoulders held back and head held high are an indication of self-confidence.

• **physical contact.** Snuggling up to you for a warm, cosy cuddle tells you immediately that your child is at ease with you and likes your company. She tells you just the opposite when she struggles furiously in your arms.

Below: At almost 2 years old, this little boy's lively expression, posture, and arm and leg movements show that he is actively engaged in an interesting game with his toy dinosaurs.

• **breathing.** Changes in your child's breathing patterns are also a clue to her state of mind – for example, rapid breathing could be a sign that she is anxious and slow, steady breathing probably means she feels good at the moment.

It's important to respond to your child's body language as well as to the words she says to you. Non-verbal communication usually

Left: This 18-month-old feels a little unsure of himself and is drawing comfort and reassurance from cuddling up to his teddy bear.

✦✦✦ Top ✦ Tips ✦✦✦

1. Get to know her. You'll get to know the hidden meaning of your toddler's body language at a faster rate if you watch her in a variety of different settings. You learn something new every time you look at her.

2. Look for similarities. The chances are that your toddler uses some of your non-verbal gestures, so try to identify these similarities. This provides a starting point for your interpretations.

3. Use her gestures yourself. This is one way to work out the meaning of her non-verbal communication. Breathe the way she breathes, scratch your head the way she does. What do you feel when you do this?

4. Be direct about it. When you are confident that you know what her body language tells you, tell her what you think. If you have misinterpreted, don't worry; and if you are spot on, your child will be pleased with you.

5. Persist. Understanding your toddler's body language takes time, and you will get better through experience. It's a case of practising until you find that you can effectively read her non-verbal messages to you.

happens without any thought behind it and is less controlled, and therefore may indicate more genuine emotions than verbal communication. When you find that you have interpreted and responded to her body language accurately – for instance, she was much happier after you cuddled her, even though she had not complained to you – this increases your confidence in your own ability to respond to your child's needs. It also increases her trust in you as a caring, loving parent.

Bear in mind that the same gesture can have different meanings in different contexts. For example, throwing a toy against the wall could indicate a range of possibilities such as pleasurable excitement, the start of a tantrum or even plain boredom. So look for clusters of gestures, perhaps involving a combination of facial expression, arm and leg movements, and body movements.

Extending Body Language

Your child's body language becomes more varied during her second and third years, for a number of reasons. First, her hand–eye coordination and movement skills become finer, enabling her to make a wider array of detailed movements and gestures. Secondly, the intensity and variety of her emotions increases and she instinctively finds more ways to communicate these to you non-verbally. Thirdly, she learns new gestures and other forms of body language from watching you and from interacting with other children her own age. For these reasons you need to watch her body language as she grows, in order to tune in to the changes.

Tantrums

Temper tantrums are common between the ages of 15 months and 3 years – research confirms that this is the peak time for such uncontrolled outbursts. Your growing child suddenly becomes unable to wait for anything, tolerate any level of frustration or hear the word 'no' without exploding with rage or erupting in tears and/or shouts. Although this is a normal, if not universal, phase of development, he needs your help to gain control over his temper.

Control

Your toddler may lose his temper at a moment's notice for many different reasons, including:

- **you ask him to stop playing with his toys so that you can tidy the room,** but he wants to continue with his game.
- **you ask him to leave the supermarket shelves alone,** but he wants to touch everything in sight.
- **he wants to sit on your knee,** yet you are too busy preparing a meal for your family.
- **he wants the pieces of the jigsaw to fit together,** but they just won't join no matter how hard he tries to make them.

The causes all have one thing in common: they are situations in which your child can't get or do what he wants. It's not that he is naughty, rather his frequent tantrums reflect his strong desire to be independent and to be able to follow his own inclinations without any barriers put in his way and to achieve any target he sets himself. In addition, he sees the world only from his point of view and hasn't yet developed to the stage where he can understand why anyone should see things differently. Over the next few years most tantrum-prone toddlers gradually learn to control their temper and become more responsive to the needs of others.

Sometimes a child has a breath-holding tantrum, in which he becomes so enraged that he involuntarily holds his breath until he faints or until his parent forces him to breathe again. Your child won't harm himself during a breath-holding tantrum, although it is frightening for you to witness. But sometimes a child inadvertently

Left: Parents can often tell from their child's expression whether a tantrum is imminent; sometimes it is possible to diffuse the situation, sometimes not.

hurts himself during a temper tantrum, when out of sheer frustration he may throw himself on the floor or bang his head off a wall or table. Make sure you watch your toddler closely when he rages in order to prevent such injuries.

Set Limits

Ironically, the best help you can give your toddler when he pushes against the limits that you have set and rages in the hope of forcing you to change your mind, is to hold your ground. You can help him gain control of his angry emotions by sticking to your decision. He needs structure and consistency in his life and it's up to you to set this for him at home. If you say 'no' but then give in to him because of his tantrum, he'll learn that a 'no' can be changed to a 'yes', if he makes a big enough fuss. And before you know it you'll have to deal with even more outbursts.

Above: Whilst not giving in to him, if you stay close and reassure him he will regain control of himself more easily.

Try not to get angry with your child when he loses his temper or when he starts to show his frustration, as that will only make matters worse. Calm him down, and explain why he can't get his own way on this occasion (whether he actually listens to you or not). If he is annoyed because he cannot complete a game or puzzle, for example, show him how to achieve this by breaking the task down into small, manageable steps. This helps him learn how to deal more effectively with his emotions.

Left: At the age of 2 the smallest setback can be enough to cause frustration and, in some cases, tears.

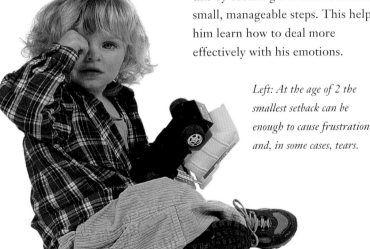

❖❖❖❖ Top·Tips ❖❖❖❖

1. Prevent the tantrum, if possible. You probably know your child well enough to spot the early warning signs, such as a reddening face, quiet moaning or irritability. If you see any indicators, distract his attention to another activity.

2. Stay calm. Your child is unlikely to regain control if you shout at him. Despite his fury – and he may even hit you during a tantrum – don't lose your own temper. By staying calm yourself, you'll help your child settle.

3. Give him reassurance. All the time that he rages, speak gently to him, telling him that everything will be all right. You may find that giving him a firm cuddle while he has a tantrum has a soothing effect on him.

4. Talk to him afterwards. Once the tantrum is over and tempers have cooled, discuss your child's behaviour with him. Explain why his actions are unacceptable and tell him that you won't give in when he behaves like that.

5. Have confidence in yourself. Remember that his tantrums are not your fault – they arise from his particular level of emotional development. Don't feel guilty, just do your best to deal with him calmly, firmly and consistently.

Eating Habits

Most toddlers pick at their food sometimes, much to the annoyance of parents. And the chances are that yours is no exception. Fussy eating might simply mean that your 15-month-old dislikes a particular food, or that your 2-year-old has a small appetite, or that your 3-year-old just likes to push her food endlessly around her plate. In any case, she will probably assert her independence on food choices from the age of about 15 months onwards. Although fussy eating is often a passing phase in a young child's life, it can also develop into a long-term characteristic. Remember that sudden loss of appetite in a child who was previously a good eater may indicate a health problem, especially if she also has other symptoms. In such cases you should seek medical advice.

Managing your Fussy Eater

There is one key point to bear in mind when tackling your toddler's mealtime habits – you can't force her to eat. No matter how much pressure you put on her, she has to make the choice to eat. This is why confrontational methods of dealing with fussy eating won't work. You need to engage your child's cooperation.

Even before you consider strategies to encourage better eating habits, think about the meal from your child's point of view. Don't forget that when you sit down at the table to eat, you expect the meal to appear enticing, to smell good and to be at the right temperature – your toddler is no different. Consider the possibility that your child may be a fussy eater because:

• **the food is too greasy.** A meal that has a high

Below: Sharing meals with the rest of the family is a social experience for a toddler and can help take the focus of attention away from what he does or does not eat.

grease content can make your child feel nauseated; other textures, such as chewy meat, can have the same effect.

• **the cutlery is the wrong size.** Small hands have a small grip, which means that cutlery suitable for your hands will be too large for your child and will therefore make eating hard work.

• **the portion is too large.** Parents often increase the size of portion they give to their child when she has a poor appetite. Smaller portions are less intimidating.

• **she can't reach the food properly.** Her chair might be too low, or she might need a cushion on it. Make sure that your child is seated so that she can reach her food comfortably and easily.

• **the food is too hot.** Temperature affects the appeal of food. Your child may prefer her food to be neither hot nor cold, just a pleasant temperature in between.

• **she dislikes the taste.** She is perfectly entitled to dislike the taste of certain foods, and you may find that her preferences differ markedly from yours.

Avoid threatening your child when she won't finish a meal. Arguments make everybody tense and anxious and this reduces her appetite even further. Stay calm, be patient and allow plenty of time for meals. Many parents are concerned about their child's poor eating because of fear that she'll miss out on vital nutrients, but this rarely happens. A basic check from your family doctor will reassure you on this point.

Eating with the Family
Remember that eating is a social experience – it's not just about your toddler satisfying her nutritional needs. The different schedules of those in your family might mean that it's more convenient for your toddler to eat on her own than to wait for everyone else. However, you may find that she enjoys eating together with the family. True, this might make the mealtime more hectic – and probably noisier as well – but your toddler learns from the eating habits of others and has more fun than when eating alone.

Another problem that can arise from your toddler eating her meal on her own is plain boredom. She is by nature sociable and she likes contact with others in the family. You can hardly blame her for, say, wanting to leave her meal and climb down from the table to play with her toys if she has no-one else to talk to while eating. This is why you should try to sit with her while she eats, at least for some of the time. She is more likely to clear her plate when you are nearby.

Below: Children love to help with cooking and there is a higher chance that your toddler will want to eat something if she has made it herself.

❖❖❖❖ Top·Tips ❖❖❖❖

1. Let your child choose. She will be more interested in eating her meal when she has been given some choice about it. If possible, let her select from a limited range of meal options so that her motivation to eat is high from the start.

2. Relax at mealtimes. Since tension is highly infectious, try to relax before serving a meal to your fussy eater. Even if you feel anxious and harassed, do your best to hide these negative feelings when your child is eating.

3. Involve her in making the meal. Although your toddler cannot cook meals herself, she could become involved in the preparation, such as bringing ingredients to you. The more she is involved, the more likely she is to eat.

4. Vary the presentation. If your child is fussy about meals served on a plate, she may be more positive about eating foods that she can pick up with her hands. Finger foods can be just as nutritious as a conventional meal and may be more appetizing to your child.

5. Praise her when she does eat. There will be times when she eats most of her meal, perhaps because she particularly liked the food. In such instances, give her lots of praise and even a small reward.

Potty Training

One of the most significant skills your child acquires between the ages of 15 months and 3 years is the ability to control his bladder and bowels. Mastering potty training is a stage in his development that gives him independence and boosts his self-confidence. However, potty training itself doesn't always go according to plan, which can result in frustration and anger for both child and parent. When that happens, progress slows considerably or may stop altogether. If you maintain a relaxed approach and avoid battles, your child will steadily gain bladder and bowel control and you will be delighted with this new phase in his development.

Think about it

Resist any temptation to start potty training before your child is ready. The fact is that your child's muscle and nervous systems won't be sufficiently mature to control his bowel and bladder until he is at least aged 15 or 16 months, and it is usually best to wait until around 20 months before beginning training. Research confirms that boys are generally slower to acquire control than girls, although nobody is sure why this gender difference exists.

If you start potty training before your toddler's ready for it, you may end up in conflict with him; you'll feel frustrated by his lack of success and his self-esteem will drop for the same reason. Potty training is most effective when there is a positive partnership between you and your child.

Right: There is no need to worry if your child is still in a nappy at night for quite a long while after he is potty trained during the day.

There are basic signs that let you know the time is right to introduce your child to the use of a potty. He may indicate to you he needs a clean nappy because he knows his nappy is wet or soiled, or he'll let you know the moment he starts to fill his nappy. Another possible sign of readiness is when you take off his nappy to change it after a few hours and you discover it is still dry. Any of these features suggest it's probably time for toilet training to begin. If you haven't spotted these signs by the time he's 2 years, start potty training anyway.

Take your Time

Make up your mind to relax about the amount of time your child takes to become potty trained. True, there are some children who gain control within a week or so of potty training actually starting, but there are also others who require several months to acquire this skill. Assume that yours will need several weeks – and if her progress is quicker, consider that a bonus! Be prepared for a mess along the way. A child who is learning bowel and bladder control almost certainly wets and soils the carpet on occasions. This is part of the learning process, so make sure you are prepared.

The first stage is to let your toddler get familiar with the potty without pressure to use it. Let him play with it so that he becomes used to this new piece of equipment. Then you can begin to persuade him to sit on it without wearing a nappy, perhaps three or four times each day. He may find this difficult as he may feel vulnerable and exposed without a nappy. Reassure him and you'll find that he gradually grows accustomed to the habit.

If you do this regularly and often enough, he is bound to wet or soil into the potty eventually. And that's the time for a fanfare of praise from you! (Bear in mind, though, that some children initially dislike what

Above: If you wait until you think your child is ready and choose a time when you are relaxed, then potty training can often be achieved within a few weeks.

they have deposited in the potty; they need to be reassured that what they have done is appropriate.) Let him see that you are delighted with his progress. It stands to reason that the more your child sits on the potty, the more successes he'll have with it. Once you've started potty training, calmly persevere no matter how long it takes. Your growing child will get there when he is ready, at his own pace. Remember that bladder control at night generally takes longer to achieve. Most children are not ready to do without a nappy at night before their third birthday.

❖❖❖ Top · Tips ❖❖❖

1. Be optimistic. Remind yourself that around 90 per cent of children manage to gain control over their bowel and bladder during the day by the age of three, and around 75 per cent have night-time control as well by that stage.

2. Choose the correct position. When using the potty, girls always take a seated position. Boys, however, have a choice when urinating – they can either sit on it or stand in front, facing it. Choose the position that you think is most suited to your child.

3. Make potty training fun. You could let your child read a book while he's perched on the potty or perhaps sing to him. If he stands up too soon, find something to attract his attention so that he continues to sit there.

4. Time the use of the potty carefully. Experience changing his used nappy has taught you when he is most likely to wet or soil. These are the best times to sit him on the potty, because success is more likely.

5. Buy trainer pants. Once your child has some bladder and bowel control, make the switch from nappies to trainer pants. Of course occasional toilet 'accidents' will continue to happen, but just clean up without a fuss.

Bedtime and Sleep

Your toddler plays a much more active part in her bedtime routine now that she's older, more independent and more able to make choices. She has her own favourite toys to accompany her and her own set way of getting ready for bed. She enjoys choosing her pyjamas and maybe even the bed covers. Your child needs to have a stable, sleeping pattern at this stage in her life – if she doesn't get a good night's sleep with regularity, she'll be tired, fractious, demanding and bad-tempered the next day. She may need help to establish good bedtime habits because she prefers to remain in your company.

Sleep Tight

Toddlers need on average about 10 hours' sleep a night, but there is considerable individual variation. You can help her settle before she goes to sleep by specifically involving her in calm, sedate activities at least 20 minutes before her bedtime routine normally begins. A predictable pre-bedtime ritual is advisable; this could be that she has a bath, puts on her pyjamas, brushes her teeth and then is read a story by you. Once this pattern becomes firmly set in her mind, she'll know that the first stage means bedtime is fast approaching.

If possible, stick to the same bedtime each night. This gets your toddler used to a fixed sleeping pattern, physically and psychologically. Of course, there will be evenings when this time varies, and that's fine. Once you

Right: If your child wakes at night, it is important to get him back to bed with the least amount of fuss; he will eventually learn that night time is for sleeping.

have tucked her in, read her a short story in a quiet voice to relax her. After that, give her a cuddle and a kiss and leave the room.

Waking Up

Research confirms that at least 15 per cent of all children around the age of 18 months still wake up regularly during the night. There are good reasons why your child might wake up and call for you during the night, perhaps because she had a bad dream, which may have been caused by a particular food or a scary story or video. When she wakes up crying, calm her and soothe her until she settles. You'll find that your reassurance helps her to get back to sleep quickly. Night terrors are different from nightmares. A child experiencing night terrors may have her eyes wide open as she sits up in bed screaming, totally convinced that the object of her fears is right there in front of her. Calm your child just as you would if she had a nightmare. Fortunately, night terrors are rare in toddlers.

Yet you may find that your toddler gradually develops the habit of night waking – and before you know it, she wakes two or three times a night without fail. To discourage this habit, keep your child in her bed when she wakes during the night. Naturally you should go to her when she cries or calls out, but try to prevent her from leaving her bedroom. If she insists on rising, say, to go to the toilet, take her back to bed as quickly as possible. Tell her that she'll soon fall asleep, and then leave the room once more. Don't go back in immediately if she calls out again – wait at least five minutes before responding to her.

There is no doubt that if your child continues to wake up and that if you then make the decision to take her downstairs for a drink or snack, or

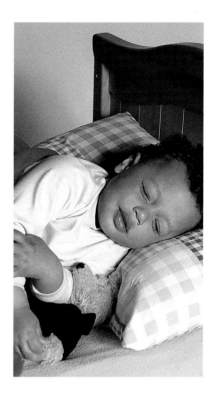

Above: If you adopt a calm and consistent approach, even a child who habitually wakes up will eventually learn to sleep through the night.

perhaps to play with her, she will probably wake up at the same time the following night, too. After all, as far as she is concerned waking up during the night is great fun – there's food, games and loads of attention from you! Of course, she may be angry with you for keeping her in the bedroom. But stick to your original plan of action. If you do, you'll discover that her waking at night soon becomes a thing of the past.

If your toddler wakes up early in the morning, encourage her to play on her own, rather than seeking your attention. Leave a pile of toys and books in the cot or by the bedside so that she can keep herself amused until you get up.

❖❖❖❖ Top·Tips ❖❖❖❖

1. Avoid naps during the day. It stands to reason that a child who sleeps during the day is less likely to sleep at night. Do what you can to keep yours awake throughout the day, even if she has sleepy moments.

2. Always take her back to her room. Be sympathetic if you find her in your bedroom in the middle of the night. But once you have calmed her, take her gently but firmly back to her own bed.

3. Don't get angry. You'll feel drained when woken by your child regularly at night because you need sleep as much as she does, but stay calm. The more excited everyone becomes, the more elusive sleep becomes.

4. Make her bedroom pleasant. She will want to spend time in her room at night when she likes what she sees there. Involve her in choosing how it is decorated, and allow her to pick the toys she wants with her. Some toddlers go to sleep more easily when a night light is left on in their room.

5. Block out potential disturbance. Loud music or the sound of a television, for instance, may keep your child awake, as might noise from outside traffic. Do what you can to reduce any disturbing noises that might keep her awake at night.

Shyness

You may be surprised to see your normally outgoing toddler become shy when he meets an unfamiliar child or adult. Suddenly, he stops talking, his face reddens and he tries to bury himself against you. It's simply a lack of social confidence that brings on this shyness – the shock of seeing an unfamiliar face or of being the focus of unwanted attention. As soon as he leaves that situation, his shyness vanishes and he becomes his usual self. Boys tend to be more shy at this age than girls (though this trend reverses after starting school).

Shyness Changes

The way children experience shyness changes as they get older. When he's 15 months, your toddler probably clings to you in the presence of someone he doesn't know. Even when within three or four months his confidence has improved and he charges about everywhere, full of his own importance and without a care in the world, he may still turn into a quivering, shy toddler if confronted by an unfamiliar face.

As his confidence gradually increases over the next six months or so, he is not so easily distressed by shyness. Of course, he may still be timid in the presence of people he doesn't know, but the panic reaction he experienced when he was slightly younger is no longer in evidence. He copes with shyness by giving a more neutral, controlled response than he did before – he is more likely to react with silence than by trying to hide. By the age of 3, he's had so much experience of meeting other children and adults that he will respond to, and sometimes initiate conversation and social interaction with strangers. Yet there will still be times when he reverts to the shy behaviour of a year or two earlier.

Be aware of the signs of shyness, because it may not be immediately obvious. When your child is feeling

Below: While the little girl on the right is happily absorbed in her drawing, the withdrawn expression of the child on the left shows that she is not at ease.

shy, he may suddenly become silent and have difficulty making eye contact with those around him – he may, for example, suddenly stare at his toes. He may be embarrassed and blush and may experience difficulty with swallowing. He may find himself rooted to the spot, unable to keep up with you, or he may struggle to get away from you. The way your child shows his

shyness depends on his individual personality, and you will soon learn to recognize the signs in his case.

Causes of Shyness

Some psychologists claim that a tendency to shyness is inherited from parents and there is some evidence to support this view. For instance, the levels of shyness of identical twins (who have almost identical genetic structures) are closer than the levels of shyness of non-identical twins (whose genetic structures are no more similar than those of ordinary siblings).

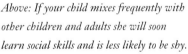

Above: If your child mixes frequently with other children and adults she will soon learn social skills and is less likely to be shy.

Other psychologists claim that shyness is affected by experience, upbringing and context. For instance, shy parents tend to have shy children, perhaps because the model of social behaviour experienced at home – which the children naturally copy – is one of shyness and so the children themselves are more likely to be shy. One study confirmed that children are more likely to be shy in an environment that values competitiveness and attainments, rather than valuing a child for his personal qualities, and this suggests the social context affects shyness. And children who live in homes where there are plenty of visitors may be less shy than those in homes where new faces are a rarity. Such findings challenge the suggestion that shyness behaviour is mainly genetic in origin.

Support

For a shy child, meeting new children and adults can be almost unbearable. Remember that his feelings are very real and that he does not behave in this way by choice. This is why it's important not to make fun of your child in the hope of cajoling him out of it; as far as he is concerned it is no laughing matter. And the thought that you might tease him makes him feel even worse. He needs your emotional support and reassurance. During an attack of shyness, a simple gesture of encouragement from you – such as a reassuring word or a calming cuddle – may be enough to lift his confidence to the point where he is able to overcome his feelings.

❖❖❖❖ Top∙Tips ❖❖❖❖

1. Don't let him avoid social situations. Your shy child might do his best to convince you, for instance, that he should not go to playgroup today because he can't face the other children. Persuade him to go along anyway.

2. Remind him of his strengths. A shy child is often convinced that the other children won't like him. So make a special point of telling him that the others will like him because, for example, he is fun to be with.

3. Give him something to do. He may not be able to think of anything to do or say when he meets other people. Suggest ideas for breaking the ice, such as telling the other child his name, or inviting the other child to play with him.

4. Teach him body language. Show your child ways to look as though he isn't shy, even though he might feel shy. Demonstrate how he should make eye contact, hold his head high and keep his hands from fidgeting nervously.

5. Provide social experience. The more your child mixes with others of his own age the greater his social confidence is likely to become and the less likely he is to feel shy when meeting new children and adults.

Confidence

Your child's self-confidence continues to grow during this phase of her life, as she learns new skills every day. She may only be young but she already has a sense of self and a sense of what she can and cannot do. Her confidence is affected by her achievements, for instance, when at the age of 15 months she manages to take the lid off a small box and empty the contents out in front of her, or at the age of 3 years when she jumps off a step and lands safely without toppling. The way others react towards her also has an impact on her level of confidence.

Components of Confidence

Self-confidence has a significant effect on your child's development because it influences her drive to achieve and her relationships with others. There are three aspects of your child's confidence to consider:

• **self-belief.** This is the extent to which she believes that she has the ability to meet the challenges that face her. A child who has little self-belief won't even try to master a

new skill because she thinks that it will be too difficult for her. As a result she would rather avoid an activity altogether than run the risk of failure.

• **self-value.** This is the extent to which your child values herself, and you'll see examples of this every day. Watch your child trying to master something – when she succeeds, she will probably turn to you and give you a huge grin. A child with a low self-value is completely unimpressed with her own achievements.

• **self-reflection.** This is the extent to which she receives positive feedback from other people around her. When you tell her how much you love her and give her a big cuddle because, say, she managed to go further up on the climbing frame than she has done before, this gives her a positive self-reflection and consequently makes her feel good about herself.

Left: A confident child will be positive and happy but it is still important to reinforce this with praise and encouragement.

A child with low self-confidence has less enjoyment in life, prefers to take a more passive role, and may have difficulty giving and receiving love from others. Challenge and adventure threaten her rather than excite her, making her reluctant to discover and learn.

Determination

Findings from psychological research suggest that a child of this age usually has strong determination and wants to achieve her goals. She is willing to explore and venture into new areas, convinced that there can be no challenge that is beyond her grasp. It's almost as though your child holds an innate positive sense of self-belief.

And this positive self-belief extends to most areas of her life. For instance, your toddler makes valiant attempts to climb the stairs in your house before she eventually succeeds, she tries to run long before she is steady enough to do this safely, and she tries to communicate with you even though she has barely started using single words. In other words, she is confident enough to try anything.

Yet her belief in herself is easily dented by experience. The sudden realization that, for example, she

❖❖❖❖ Top·Tips ❖❖❖❖

1. Have plenty of loving physical contact. A warm, loving hug is a very fundamental way of telling your child that you love her and that you think she is marvellous. This sort of contact with you boosts her self-belief.

2. Reassure her. If she explodes with frustration because, for example, she can't fit all the pieces of the jigsaw together, try to calm her. Reassure her that she'll soon master it, and then on this occasion solve the puzzle for her.

3. Break challenges into small stages. Your child wants to do everything, even when the task is beyond her. Help her complete a new activity in stages, each of which is a separate achievement. For example, encourage her to run a few steps at first before she attempts to race across the room.

4. Tell your child what you feel about her. Your praise and encouragement has a huge positive effect on her self-confidence. She values your attention and is proud when you comment on her achievements. She never tires of receiving your praise.

5. Avoid obvious pitfalls. There is no point in deliberately letting your child learn through failure. If you know that she is heading for a disappointment, steer her away from that activity before she gets fully involved.

Above: This toddler's relaxed stance and confident stride show her self-belief as she tries a new piece of playground equipment.

can't place all the shapes into the shape-sorter can dampen her interest in the toy. The same thing can happen when your child tries to propel her three-wheeler using the pedals, discovers that she hasn't moved it at all, and then cries in frustration. If failure of this sort occurs often enough, your child's self-confidence dips and she'll give up trying.

So watch her closely when she plays. Give her the freedom to play on her own in order that she feels the success of achievement, yet at the same time be ready to step in if you see disappointment and frustration building up. And if your child does lose her temper or let frustration get the better of her, cuddle her, cheer her up and direct her towards another toy or activity that you know she has already mastered. She can always return to the original activity later when she is in a more positive frame of mind.

Special Needs

Estimates suggest that up to one child in five has special needs – in other words, his development does not follow the typical pattern. For instance, his speech might not develop at the same rate as that of other children his age, he may still not have taken his first step long after his peers are steady on their feet, or he might not understand how to use a particular toy even though it has been designed for use by his age group. A child with special needs has the same emotional needs as any other child but he has special needs when it comes to stimulation.

Identification

Some developmental problems are not spotted until a child is at least 15 months old, for example, when the child doesn't start to talk at the time he is expected to or because his understanding seems less advanced than would typically be expected of a child his age. If you have any doubts at all about your child's development, speak to your family doctor or other health professional. The chances are that you have no need to be worried, but you'll feel reassured by an informed opinion from someone else.

The developmental checklists given later in this chapter offer a guide to typical progress made between the ages of 15 months and 3 years. Do remember, however, that if your child does not pass the stages by the suggested times, it does not mean he has special needs. He'll probably

Right: Even though a child with special needs may not progress at the same rate as other children of his age, he will enjoy and learn from social contact.

be ready to progress to the next skill very soon and just needs a little time to develop his potential.

It is obviously a source of worry to discover that your child has special needs. Some parents blame themselves even though they are clearly not at fault and may feel guilty. It's helpful to share these feelings with a friend or partner who can lend a sympathetic, understanding ear. Professional counselling may be appropriate for families of children with severe developmental problems.

Above: It is important for all children, whether with special needs or not, to be allowed to progress at their own pace.

The Importance of Play

Your child with special needs still learns through play – it is as important to him as it is for any other child. However, he may need additional help in order to get the most out of the stimulation you provide for him. Monitor his play patterns and his reactions to toys and other stimulation activities in order to discover the most effective ways of engaging his interest and promoting progress.

Take a positive outlook. For every difficulty and hurdle your child experiences when playing, there is a practical solution. For instance:

• **make more of an effort to stimulate his interest,** by showing him a wider array of toys and by playing with him for longer.

• **he has limited concentration and loses interest quickly.** Play with him for shorter periods but have more play sessions during the day. His concentration is sharper when he uses it in shorter bursts.

• **he has weak hand control and can't hold toys properly in his fingers.** Gently ease his fingers open, place the toy in the palm of his hand and gently wrap his fingers around it. This gives him the feeling of opening and closing his hands.

• **his language development is slower than expected and he still doesn't seem to be able to combine two words to make a phrase.** Continue to stimulate his language by talking with him, singing nursery rhymes and songs together, and looking at books with him.

• **his slower physical development restricts his ability to move and find objects of interest.** Identify the toys and other items that attract his attention and bring them to him. This overcomes the learning limitation placed on him by his restricted physical abilities.

Get to know your child's strengths and weaknesses so that you can devise appropriate play strategies. Although his progress may be slower than you might expect, given plenty of stimulation he will advance and improve his abilities during his second and third years.

Development
Movement

- Walks unsteadily with support up and down stairs. Some toddlers may use different strategies such as crawling or going down on their bottom.
- Walks confidently about the home and outside.
- Picks up toys or other objects from the floor without toppling over.
- Trots towards you across the room, but may become unsteady if she starts to run.
- Starts to climb playground equipment, but will need constant supervision.
- May enjoy splashing and kicking in the swimming pool.

Hand–Eye Coordination

- Sees a connection between her hand movements and the effect this causes. For example, she pulls at a string to make the attached toy move towards her.
- Enjoys making random marks on paper using crayons or paints.
- Starts to feed herself with her hands and a spoon.
- Holds two small items in each hand at the same time.
- May want to help dress herself.
- Hand preference may become apparent.
- Claps her hands together.
- Successfully completes a simple inset board activity.

Language

- Is able to follow and act on simple instructions.
- Consistently uses approximately six or seven words, but her understanding extends to many more words.
- Combines language and gestures to express her needs.
- Starts to learn the names of different parts of the body.
- Enjoys songs and nursery rhymes and will perhaps join in with some sounds and actions.

15–18 Month Skills

Learning

- Combines the use of different skills and capacities, such as concentration, memory, hand–eye control and understanding, to complete a complex task such as a simple inset board.
- Solves simple problems like removing the lid from a box to see inside.
- Learns the basic concepts of quantities and volume through water play.
- Improved attention span enables her to concentrate on and complete more demanding activities.
- Understands and follows stories that are read to her and responds to familiar characters.
- Remembers where she put an item that interests her, such as a favourite toy.

Social and Emotional

- May have a tantrum when she doesn't get her own way as she begins to assert her sense of independence.
- Wants to do more for herself, especially with feeding and dressing.
- Learns good eating habits by sharing mealtimes.
- Begins to learn basic social skills like passing a toy to another child.
- Plays alongside other children, watching them closely, and learns by taking in how they interact and play with toys.
- Expresses preferences for particular foods or for certain toys that she wants to play with.
- May become jealous when you pay attention to others.

Development

Movement

- Is able to undertake another activity while he is on the move. For example, he can trail a pull-along toy behind him as he walks.
- Likes to clamber over furniture.
- Climbs up and down from a chair.
- Improved balance and coordination leads to fewer instances of tripping over and unexpected falls when he is walking and running.
- Is able to use a wider range of playground equipment.
- Enjoys running freely in a park and in the garden.

Hand–Eye Coordination

- Enjoys playing with modelling materials like play doh or clay, and sand and water – making shapes and drawing 'pictures' into the surface.
- Likes rolling, throwing and perhaps even catching balls, both large and small, though he will find large ones easier to grasp.
- Stacks small wooden blocks on top of each other to make a tower of perhaps five bricks.
- Pours water accurately from one container into another one without too much splashing.
- Makes increasingly deliberate marks on paper with a crayon.

Language

- Has extended his vocabulary to dozens of words, mostly nouns that describe a general class of object such as 'car' for all vehicles or 'house' for all buildings.
- Tries to join in songs.
- Is interested in conversations and begins to learn conversational conventions, such as giving and waiting for answers.

- Puts words together to form two-word phrases.
- Develops an understanding that speech is about social contact as well as communicating basic needs.
- Spots familiar characters and objects in picture books and photographs and tries to name them.

19–21 Month Skills

Learning

Begins to use toys for imaginative play, as a result of his developing capacity for symbolic thought.

His increasing problem-solving ability enables him to complete a simple inset board and these toys are now well within his capability.

His developing curiosity makes him want to see what goes on outside and to explore closed cupboards.

Uses all his senses, including sight, hearing and touch, to learn about the world in which he lives and becomes more confident in exploring new environments.

Becomes more focused and determined and is more motivated to complete a challenging task.

Social and Emotional

Appreciates your company and makes an effort to engage your attention either through talk or play.

Can walk backwards a few steps.

Shows that he is nearly ready to begin potty training, although full control is unlikely at this age.

Persists in challenging decisions that he disagrees with.

Begins to interact with other children but needs lots of basic social guidance.

Is able to understand simple rules, although he may not always comply with them.

Enjoys the security of a regular daily routine.

Development
Movement

- Pushes a pedal toy along with her feet, though probably cannot yet turn the pedals.
- Can stand on one foot while using the other to kick a ball.
- Runs confidently and rarely falls, although this activity still requires quite a lot of concentration.
- Moves fast as long as she goes in a straight line.
- Is able to throw and catch a ball from a sitting position.
- Dances to music.
- Can adjust her balance well on a swing.

Hand–Eye Coordination

- Looks at books for several minutes studying each picture, pointing to images that catch her interest and turning the pages.
- Can participate increasingly in helping to dress and undress herself.
- Combines her index finger and thumb effectively in the pincer grip to pick up small objects.
- Receives and passes objects from your hand to hers and then back again.
- Makes increasingly rhythmic sounds with simple musical instruments such as drums and tambourines.

Language

- Accurately identifies everyday objects placed in front of her.
- Experiments with different (perhaps 'incorrect') word combinations.
- Tackles most sounds but often mixes up or mispronounces certain consonants such as 'c' or 's'.
- Names the main parts of her body.

- Listens with interest to other people talking to each other.
- Her vocabulary is at least 200 words, often combined in short sentences.

22–24 Month Skills

Learning

Understands that she can manipulate objects to learn more about them. For example, she twists objects to see inside them.

Is enthusiastic about imaginative play, creating stories and scenes using toys, such as figures, to act them out.

Watches you closely then copies you as a way of learning new skills.

Has an unquenchable thirst for information and asks lots of questions about everything around her.

Is increasingly able to understand explanations.

Will be able to remember and recount some past events.

Social and Emotional

- Enjoys the company of other children, but has trouble sharing her toys and does not yet play cooperatively.
- Is able to feed herself with a spoon effectively.
- Potty training is probably underway but her bladder and bowel control may not yet be totally reliable.
- Wants to help wash herself at bathtime and clean her teeth.
- Enjoys the responsibility of carrying out small tasks.
- May cry when separated from you temporarily, although she soon stops when you are out of sight.
- May be shy with strangers.

Development
Movement

- Is able to jump a short distance off the ground from a standing position and with practice may be able to jump over a low obstacle.
- Successfully manoeuvres himself around obstacles while performing another task. For example, he can push a toy wheelbarrow around the room without crashing into the furniture.
- Is able to take short walks on foot rather than using the buggy.
- Walks up stairs in your house without your support.
- Stands on tiptoes for a couple of seconds.

Hand–Eye Coordination

- Manages to thread large beads onto a lace.
- When painting and drawing grips the crayon or brush with his fingers and is able to make a controlled mark. For example, he may be able to copy a vertical line that you have drawn.
- Copes better with construction toys and games and puzzles that have pieces that fit together.
- Can do up and undo large buttons.
- Can start to learn how to use pieces of cutlery other than his spoon.
- Has firmly established hand preference.

Language

- Adores you reading stories to him just before he goes to sleep.
- Benefits from discussing his activities with you and will get more out of a television programme, for example, if you talk about it afterwards.
- Asks questions and listens attentively to the answers.
- Has a vocabulary of several hundred individual words.

- Enjoys simple conversations with familiar adults and other children.
- Uses language to extend the complexity of imaginative play, such as dressing up.
- Starts to use pronouns, such as 'he' or 'you' and prepositions, such as 'in' or 'on'.
- Recalls small amounts of personal information, such as his age and full name, and is able to relate that information.

25–30 Month Skills

Learning

Begins to match colours, for example, by finding two bricks of the same colour.

Understands that coins are 'money', but still has little concept of their value.

Sorts objects according to specific characteristics. He is able for example, to divide toys according to type – say, animals or cars.

Begins to develop a broad sense of time. For example he can probably distinguish between 'today' and 'tomorrow'.

Identifies himself in a photograph shown to him.

Is hungry for new experiences beyond the home and enjoys visits to new places such as the zoo.

• Ascribes human qualities to inanimate objects as an expression of his active imagination and perhaps as a means of understanding the world around him. For example, he may be worried that a favourite toy will be sad if he leaves it at home.

Social and Emotional

• May still be 'clingy' when you leave him in someone else's care.

• Starts to learn basic social skills, such as sharing, when playing with siblings and other children.

• Takes an increasingly active part in dressing and undressing. He may pull off his socks and jumper when getting ready for bed.

• Is more keen to play with other children at times, although arguments are still common.

• Insists on trying more things on his own but may become despondent when he experiences frustration and failure.

• Is prone to tantrums when things don't go his way.

Development
Movement

- Jumps from a small height, such as a single step, without losing her balance.
- Will attempt challenging balancing activities such as walking along a log or hopping, although she may not succeed.
- Balances for several seconds while standing on one foot only.
- Tiptoes across the floor without over-balancing.
- Is able to negotiate ladders and slides on large outdoor play equipment.
- Runs fast with great confidence.
- Can use the pedals of a pedal toy to propel herself along.
- Can accurately copy movements and participates fully in action songs.

Hand–Eye Coordination

- Benefits from the wider range of play equipment and craft activities at a playgroup or nursery.
- Can build a tower of eight or more blocks.
- Begins to be able to cut paper with a pair of child-safe scissors, although she finds this difficult.
- Completes simple jigsaw puzzles.
- Due to improved control, her drawings are less random and their subject is often recognizable. She can copy simple shapes you draw.
- Carries out simple household tasks like putting cutlery on the table or toys in a box.

Language

- Issues instructions confidently to you.
- Frequently uses pronouns such as 'I', and 'me', although not always correctly.
- Has a vocabulary of at least a thousand words.
- Is ready for more complex stories with multiple characters.

- Asks frequent questions about the meaning of unfamiliar words that she has heard you or others use.
- Shows an understanding of grammatical rules, which she applies in her use of language.

31–36 Month Skills

Learning

- Compares two objects in terms of size or height, albeit not always accurately.
- Makes up simple stories from her imagination.
- Remembers something you both did yesterday and may be able to recall exciting events in the more distant past.
- Anticipates the consequences of her actions. For example, she knows that if she knocks her cup over the drink will spill.
- Completes jigsaws with three or four large pieces.
- Is able to commit information, such as the name of an object, to memory by repeating it to herself.

Social and Emotional

Has a distinct sense of self and is protective of her possessions and personal space.

Is reliably clean and dry during the day.

May form a special friendship with one child in particular.

More aware of other people's feelings and makes efforts to offer help and comfort to another child who is distressed.

Becomes more confident in new situations and in forming relationships outside the immediate family.

Is more amenable to family rules and tantrums diminish in frequency.

Enjoys exercising choice over what to eat or wear.

Movement

The Development of Movement

During the period from 15 months to 3 years, your child's physical capabilities progress from being able to 'toddle' around unsteadily on his feet – having only recently taken his first few walking steps – into confident mastery of a broad range of complex physical skills, such as throwing, catching, running, balancing and kicking. Of course, his movement skills continue to develop in subsequent years but it is during this phase of his life that these advanced physical abilities begin to emerge.

Foundation for Change

The foundation for your growing child's better control over his arms, legs, body, balance and coordination stems from three sources. First, the seeds of these abilities have been sown in the previous 15 months, as your baby's coordination steadily improved from his original random arm and leg movements at birth into purposeful actions.

The second source is the stimulation you gave your baby as he steadily gained mastery over basic physical movements like rolling from his tummy onto his back and vice versa, using his arms and legs to crawl from one side of the room to the other, and eventually standing independently without support. He continues to need your encouragement in order to maintain his progress with coordination skills.

The third major source of his ever-improving movement skills is the physical changes that occur in his second and third years. Here are some of the changes that take place:

• **height and weight.** By around the age of 2 years, your child has probably attained half the height that he will be as an adult, and his weight has also increased. His legs are longer and his muscles are stronger and firmer, enabling him to move in a more agile manner, at a greater speed, and with more purposeful actions.

• **brain.** At birth, your child's brain was approximately 25 per cent of its eventual adult weight, while at the age of 2 years his brain has grown to approximately 75 per cent of its full adult weight. And this increased brain size is accompanied by

maturation in part of the lower brain (called the cerebellum), giving him more control over his balance and posture.

• **vision.** Another effect of the brain maturation that occurs in your child's second and third years is that his vision improves and he is able to focus his sight more accurately. To tackle effectively movement challenges such as climbing, running, throwing and balancing, your child must be able to use his vision continually to scan the area in front of him. He is much better able to do this by the time he is this age.

Right: By the age 2 of your toddler is likely to be walking confidently.

Left: He will be steady enough on his feet to carry bulky objects and manage steps without support.

Above: This 18-month-old boy has mastered throwing a ball. This kind of skill comes naturally to some children while others take longer to learn it.

My Child is Clumsy

There is huge variation in the rate at which children acquire coordination skills. You need only to watch a group of 2- or 3-year-olds to see that some are more agile than others. So there is no need to worry if yours is always the one who seems to trip most or who is last to manoeuvre himself onto the first step of the climbing frame – individual differences in the development of movement are perfectly normal.

Statistics reveal, however, that between five and seven per cent of young children are clumsy, in other words, they have difficulty with every activity involving arm, leg and body movements. Anything involving balance and coordination proves to be an overwhelming challenge for a clumsy child. The ratio of clumsy boys to clumsy girls is about 2:1.

The dividing line between a child who is slow to acquire new coordination abilities and a child who is clumsy is unclear. This lack of a clear definition doesn't really matter because every child – clumsy, average or agile – requires stimulation and encouragement to improve. Bear in mind that the root of clumsiness lies in the way the child perceives the world and in the way he is able to coordinate a number of processes – it is not due to any physical problem with his arms or legs.

The biggest hurdle facing a clumsy child – and in fact any child who struggles with a physical challenge – is that he may lose confidence in himself and may start to give up too easily when it comes to movement activities. A child with poor coordination often expects to fail and so doesn't try hard. He needs your support to overcome the difficulties he experiences so that he can maintain his self-confidence and continue to enjoy healthy physical play.

Safety

Now that your child is able to tackle a wider range of physical activities – either inside the home or outside, perhaps in the garden or in a park or playground – safety must remain a priority. As the coordination challenges he wants to tackle become more complex, the potential hazards he faces also begin to increase.

Aside from the obvious safeguard of keeping an eye on your roving child, carefully check all outdoor equipment. Buy climbing frames, slides and swings only from reputable toy suppliers, and make sure that the equipment is firmly assembled according to the manufacturers' instructions. Apply the same safety criteria to play apparatus in playgrounds and parks. Look at the equipment for potential hazards before you let your child play on it – if you are in any doubt, take him elsewhere to play.

Below: Children at this age have no real sense of danger and can get themselves into difficulties so make your child's safety a priority at all times.

Movement

Age	Skill
15–18 months	Her improved balance and posture allow her to see something on the floor, and then to pick it up without toppling over.
	Stairs continue to fascinate your child, but her unreliable balance and lack of agility mean that she needs your supervision when going up and down them.
	She can move reasonably quickly and comfortably about the house, though she's not entirely stable when she tries to go faster.
	Likes to splash around in water, but may become anxious if the area is too crowded or the water is too wavy.
19–21 months	Your child's new climbing skills give her enough confidence to explore new places and to try to clamber over household furniture.
	Instances of tripping over and unexpected falls as she walks and runs decrease significantly – a result of better balance, coordination and an improvement in her confidence.
	Her movement ability has advanced to the point where she can effectively complete more than one physical activity at the same time, without becoming confused.
22–24 months	She is much steadier on her feet and she rarely falls, even while running. However, she still needs to concentrate hard when moving quickly.

From 15 Months to 3 Years

What to Do

When she is standing, let her see you take a small toy over to her. Pass it towards her and just as she reaches for the toy, let it 'accidentally' slip from your hand on to the floor. She will slowly bend down, take hold of the item, then stand upright again.

Stand beside your toddler at the bottom of a flight of stairs and hold her hand. Encourage her to walk with you slowly, one step at a time. Gripping your hand, she'll lift a foot on to the first step and then the other foot on to the same step.

Encourage your toddler to walk at every opportunity; resist the temptation to carry her in order to complete a journey quicker. Ask her to trot towards you across the room – running may be too difficult – and cuddle her when she tries to do this.

At first, let her splash around in the small pool at your local swimming centre. Make sure she has a buoyancy aid securely around her, and stay beside her at all times for her safety and confidence. You may decide to join a toddler's swimming class.

Teach her how to get into a chair. If it is a child-sized seat, she will soon learn how to approach it, turn around, and slide backwards into it. If it is a standard easy chair, she will be able to climb into it, before turning herself around and sitting back in it.

Watch your child closely as she runs freely around the home. When you see her start to topple, remind her to slow down, to take her time and to look in front of her whenever she moves. These simple prompts reduce the number of falls.

Give her a pull-along toy, the type on wheels attached to a long piece of string. Your child can walk along while pulling this toy beside or behind her. The toy does not distract her or force her off-balance while walking.

On an outing to the park, find a flat, grassy area and ask your child to run alongside you. she will be able to move fast as long as she goes in a straight line – making quick changes of direction or turning corners forces her to slow down to avoid stumbling.

Movement

Age	Skill
	She begins to be able to stand on one foot for a second or so, while using the other foot to kick a ball.
	Pedal toys provide your child with much amusement, even though she is not yet able to turn the pedals herself.
25–30 months	Your child's balance, muscular strength and limb coordination is sufficient for her to make a reasonable attempt at jumping off the ground from a standing position.
	Your child can coordinate her arm and leg movements to move herself around the room without bumping into things, while concentrating on another task at the same time.
	Her increased confidence and movement skills mean that she wants to negotiate the flight of stairs in your house entirely on her own, without you beside her.
31–36 months	Your child's jumping ability has improved, and she is able to jump off small heights without losing her balance when she lands on the ground.
	Your child's balance and coordination has improved to the point where she can confidently and accurately complete complex physical activities which previously were too difficult.
	She adores any opportunity to use large outdoor play equipment, especially when she knows you are watching her. She is proud of her achievements on large apparatus.

From 15 Months to 3 Years

What to Do

Stand your child a few metres away, facing you, and place a large ball at her feet. Ask her to kick the ball to you. At first, she may lose her balance as she tries to do this, but with practice she eventually kicks it while remaining upright.

Give her a small sit-on toy that has wheels and also pedals. Make sure the seat is low enough for your child to be able to place her feet firmly on the ground. She can't turn the pedals but she tries to push herself along by pressing her feet on the ground.

Demonstrate to your child how you can jump off the ground, with both feet together. She will try to imitate you, though she probably won't use her arms to balance and propel herself like you. This is a difficult task, but she'll enjoy attempting it.

If your child has a large wheeled toy, such as a plastic wheelbarrow, she can hold it firmly in her hands and push it around your house without crashing into the furniture all the time and without tripping up. Remind her to concentrate as she moves.

Stand at the bottom of the stairs and watch your child start to climb them on her own. She may be a little nervous and needs to hold on with one hand either to the banister or against the wall itself as she ascends – she should not look back at you until the top.

Ask your child to stand on the bottom step of a flight of stairs, facing the downwards direction. She will be able to jump off towards you with both feet, making a safe and steady landing. As her confidence grows, she will try to jump off the second step, too.

You'll find that she can balance for several seconds while standing on one foot only, with the other foot raised from the ground. She is also steadier on toes and can tiptoe her way across the floor without over-balancing or putting her feet flat on the ground.

Your child delights in climbing up the small ladder, then using the slide to get to the bottom. She is more adventurous on the climbing frame, and tries to keep the swing in motion after a push start. Hold her hand when she's balancing on a fixed log.

Stimulating Movement: 15 to 18 Months

Your child becomes increasingly adventurous as his confidence in his ability to move grows. His natural curiosity, coupled with his new coordination skills, opens up a whole new range of play experiences for him. He realizes that he can move around much more easily without needing to seek help and struts about the house full of self-importance.

CHANGES IN WALKING STYLE
One of the things you'll notice is that your toddler's style of walking changes. And it's not just that he grows steadier on his feet as he approaches 18 months. When he walks his toes tend to point towards the front rather than inwards (which enables him to move at a quicker rate).

He also keeps his feet closer to the ground instead of lifting them as high as he did when he took his first steps (which helps him maintain balance) and he takes shorter steps. The combination of all these small changes results in improved stability and control while walking.

Suitable Suggestions

Toddlers have an amazing ability to improvise – for example, they go up and down stairs using a variety of different strategies, ranging from crawling on all fours to bottom-shuffling their way from stair to stair. There is no 'right' way to do this; your toddler will use the technique that best suits him and his level of physical development. The best help you can give is plenty of encouragement, because his enthusiasm can quickly be dampened by repeated failure, perhaps because he can't coordinate his feet well enough or because every time he bends down he falls over. When success eludes him, he may be tempted to give up trying completely.

That's why your presence can be extremely supportive, not just in giving your toddler verbal support but also in providing practical help. For example, you could hold his hand when he attempts to walk quickly – in this way you both know that there is no risk of him toppling over, and therefore he'll be prepared to try harder. Or you could form your hands into a protective cage around your child – without your hands actually

Right: Give your child plenty of encouragement to take on challenges like climbing stairs. Keep your hands close to him to prevent a fall.

touching him – as he does his best to climb up a set of steps.

Your presence gives him a feeling of safety as well as increasing his sense of delight in his achievements as he shares them with you. This boosts his self-confidence, motivating him to repeat the experience. Of course, your intention should be to reduce this level

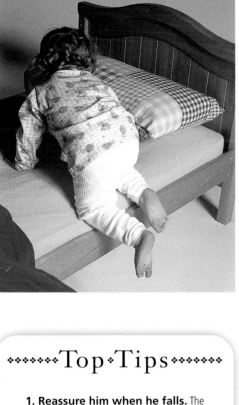

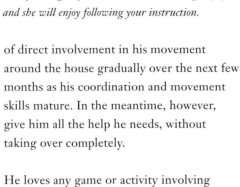

Left: Encourage your toddler to fulfil simple tasks for herself. It is good for her to learn to do things safely and she will enjoy following your instruction.

of direct involvement in his movement around the house gradually over the next few months as his coordination and movement skills mature. In the meantime, however, give him all the help he needs, without taking over completely.

He loves any game or activity involving movement and these let him get used to the sensations associated with changing posture and position. Your toddler squeals with delight when you and he recite action songs together and do the movements in synchrony. Try to learn a varied repertoire of these songs, for example, from other parents, books and videos.

✦✦✦✦✦✦✦ Top ✦ Tips ✦✦✦✦✦✦✦

1. Reassure him when he falls. The occasional tumble may upset him. All it takes to get him on his feet again is a cuddle from you, and reassurance that he is unlikely to fall again.

2. Demonstrate actions if necessary. Your toddler learns by experience and he may need you to show him, for instance, how to sit in a large chair. He watches you closely and then tries to do the same himself.

3. Calm his anxiety. He may become frustrated, for example, when the pull-along toy doesn't go in the exact direction he wants. Don't let him give up. Instead, calm him and then encourage him to continue pulling the toy as he walks.

4. Don't do everything for him. It's a lot easier and quicker when, for instance, you lift him into his chair. But he won't learn how to do this himself if that becomes your regular habit. He needs to try these manoeuvres on his own.

5. Make him aware of safety. Your toddler's new level of exploration skills potentially places him at higher risk. Remind him to take care and to watch what he does, but don't overdo the warnings or he may become unnecessarily fearful.

Above: At this age toddlers frequently fall and bump themselves as they are trying out new moves. Your comfort and encouragement will help your child through this phase.

M O V E M E N T

Q&A

Q Do socks and shoes give my toddler confidence with walking?

A For outside the house, your toddler needs to wear socks and shoes to protect his feet. Inside the house, however, his movement skills will be helped by letting him toddle about in his bare feet. This gives his foot muscles maximum grip on the floor and allows him to use his toes more effectively for maintaining balance.

Q My toddler looks as though he has a fat tummy. Could this slow his progress with movement?

A At this age your child's liver is very large in proportion to his overall body size and also his bladder is still quite high in the abdomen. These physical characteristics may make you think he is overweight – even though he is not – and they have no negative effect at all on his movement.

🧸🚚 **Toys:** pull-along toy, sit-and-ride toy, child-sized table and chair, inflatable soft balls, paddling pool

Stimulating Movement: 19 to 21 Months

The most significant change in your toddler's movement skills at this stage is her ability to move around while completing another activity at the same time. For instance, she can pull a toy behind her as she walks. Previously, the basic act of coordinating her arm, leg and body movements was so demanding that she required her full concentration on that activity alone.

MASTERY THROUGH REPETITION

Don't be surprised to find your child going over the same movement experience again and again – this is her instinctive way of mastering a new skill. For example, you may discover your 21-month-old climbing up on to a chair so that she can sit at the table, then immediately climbing down again, followed by a further attempt to climb up again.

It's not that she is easily amused or that she can't think of anything else to do. She instinctively knows that repetition is the best way to improve her movement, balance and coordination, and she keeps going until she feels that she has got it right.

Left: Once your child is really steady on his feet he can master more playground equipment which in turn will help him improve his strength and coordination.

gets all the practice she needs. She can climb on to the sofa alongside you while you read her a story in the morning or afternoon, she can scale the heights of a kitchen chair to watch you set out the table for the evening meal, and she can walk freely in the garden while you are out there, too. Utilizing everyday activities as they arise spontaneously ensures that she has ample opportunity to consolidate and enhance her coordination, balance and movement.

Suitable Suggestions

Although your growing child might be happy to sit herself down in front of the television or video for most of the day, for the benefit of her health and development make sure that there is plenty of physical activity in her daily routine. Encourage her to get involved with your own schedule, so that, for instance, she walks along the aisles of the supermarket with you or she follows you up and down stairs. The more movement activities she has, the better.

And you don't have to construct any specific physical exercises for her. Just following you around during the day will ensure that she

Below: At this age toddlers can complete more complex tasks like using a spade to fill a bucket with sand.

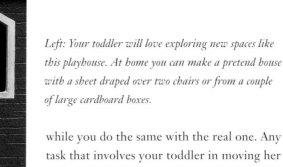

Begin to give her simple movement challenges that have more than one element in them. For instance, you could ask her to go over to the other side of the room, pick up the toy that is lying there and put it back into the toy box in the far corner. Or she can push her toy vacuum cleaner across the floor

Left: Your toddler will love exploring new spaces like this playhouse. At home you can make a pretend house with a sheet draped over two chairs or from a couple of large cardboard boxes.

while you do the same with the real one. Any task that involves your toddler in moving her body from one place to the next, while simultaneously carrying out another physical activity, automatically benefits the development of her movement and coordination skills.

Your toddler loves showing off her new talents to you, whether it's climbing up stairs or running at a pace which she thinks is fast. This is why she asks you to watch her as she demonstrates each new achievement. Even though the task she is engaged in is perhaps beyond her, she is so proud of her newly acquired skills that she wants your approval. And when you smile at her effort, you are encouraging her to persevere until she achieves her goal.

Below: Your child will now be able to play independently on some moving toys and will gain an enormous sense of achievement from this.

✧✧✧✧✧✧✧ Top·Tips ✧✧✧✧✧✧✧

1. Let her roam freely. Your toddler needs freedom to explore and to move around in the way she wants in order to test out her new skills. As long as you know that she is safe, allow her to venture around your house without restricting her too much.

2. Offer solutions. She may not be able immediately to spot the solution to the movement challenge facing her. If she struggles unsuccessfully at an activity, suggest ways that she could achieve her target – she will respond to your ideas.

3. Take your toddler to the park. Even if your local park has no play equipment for young children, she will adore playing on wide open, grassy areas. She knows that if she falls on the grass, she won't hurt herself.

4. Regularly rearrange her furniture. For instance, you might decide to put her chair at the opposite side of the table today. This means she has to use her movement skills in a slightly different way in order to climb into a sitting position.

5. Practise walking and stopping with her. You have great fun together as you teach her how to stop quickly. At first, she will need several steps before she can bring herself to a standstill from walking fast, but she soon gets better at this.

Q&A

Q Should she be able to walk backwards at this age?

A Most children can manage this by 21 months, though it can take time to learn. When your toddler faces you, she can probably take steps to go backwards, but if she half turns around to look over her shoulder as she moves in the reverse direction, she may tumble over. She should practise this on a carpeted floor.

Q Could a toddler climb up so high that she could open a latch on a window?

A Yes. You'd be amazed how skilful an active child can be in moving pieces of furniture together so that she can reach new heights – your child is very creative when it comes to problem-solving like this. Install childproof locks on your windows, especially if you have rooms above ground-floor level.

Toys: tricycle with large pedals, child-sized furniture, plastic gardening tools, pull-along toy that makes a noise when moved

Stimulating Movement: 22 to 24 Months

Your child's improved balance and body movements, coupled with his increased chest, hips and leg strength, give him the ability and confidence to attempt physical tasks that he could previously observe only passively, such as running, jumping, kicking, throwing and catching. Naturally, he is still in the early stages of acquiring these particular skills, but he will make steady progress over the next few months.

PHYSICAL MATURATION

There is wide variation in athletic ability among 2-year-olds. This is largely due to different rates of physical and neurological maturation. For your toddler to achieve complex movement skills, he must have developed the important underlying muscular and neurological structures. If his development hasn't reached this point, he won't be able to master skills like running, throwing and climbing, no matter how much he practises these actions. So be careful not to push your child too hard if he struggles physically – it's probably that his body just isn't ready. Try again in a few weeks.

Suitable Suggestions

Ball games can start to figure more, as he is better able to coordinate his hands and feet. Have a range of balls of various sizes for him to play with. When he tries to kick a ball, you might find that he sometimes falls when he swings his leg – his balance during this sort of activity remains shaky – but mostly he remains standing. Encourage him to keep the upper half of his body steady while he kicks at the ball because this helps to keep his centre of gravity between his feet.

Kicking from a standing position is the easiest way for your toddler to get started – kicking from a moving position is altogether more demanding for an enthusiastic 2-year-old. The chances are that when he first tries to walk up to a ball and kick it without stopping, he'll simply trip over it! Pick him up, dust him down, wipe away any tears, and suggest he tries again. He needs plenty of practice.

Left: At around 2 years children will enjoy learning to kick a ball to you, though a fluid kicking action will generally take a while to master.

Gradually he will learn either to stop completely before he kicks the ball or to time his steps so that he can swing his leg at the ball without having to change stride. This is a complex skill that takes time to achieve. Make sure that your toddler has fun during these games; he'll lose interest if it becomes too serious.

The same applies to the actions of throwing and catching. The lower your child's bottom is to the ground, the easier it is for him to throw and catch a ball (because his centre of gravity is lower, which in turn increases his stability). Practise both throwing and catching while he sits on the ground and use

Right: Toddlers love dancing and jumping around to music and it is a great way of expending excess energy on a rainy day.

a medium-sized ball that he can grasp easily. If you find that your child can manage these actions successfully from that position, he's ready to try catching and throwing while in a standing position. Be prepared for your toddler to fall a few times, as his attempts to catch and throw push him off balance. Again, regular practice is the key to mastering these skills.

Below: Riding around on his tricycle will give your toddler a real sense of independence although at this age he may push himself along rather than using the pedals.

❖❖❖❖❖❖❖ Top · Tips ❖❖❖❖❖❖❖

1. Play with him on a swing. He enjoys the sensations of moving backwards and forwards on a swing, as long as he is securely fastened and cannot slip off. He learns to adjust his balance continually as the swing moves in each direction.

2. Listen to music with him. Your toddler will happily dance to the rhythm of the music of his favourite song. And he will try to imitate any dancer that he sees on television. His enthusiasm increases if you dance along with him.

3. Provide success. Have realistic expectations of your child's progress. He needs to experience success in activities involving movement or his motivation will soon diminish. When he does achieve something new, let him know how thrilled you are.

4. Expect occasional lulls in his progress. There will be temporary phases during which he makes almost no advance in his movement skills. This happens with most children. He will start to progress once again when he is ready for change.

5. Promote his independence. Your child is now at the age where he likes to do things for himself and you should encourage this. He doesn't need you to fetch and carry for him – he can cope with many physical activities on his own.

Q Will dancing improve my child's movement?

A There's nothing like dancing to music for getting a toddler to twist and turn his body. The dance won't be systematic or follow any set pattern, but it will require lots of movement, plenty of coordination, and loads of balance. This is a great way for your child to develop his agility while also having fun.

Q Is it true that 2-year-old boys are usually taller than 2-year-old girls and so are generally more athletic?

A It is true that by the age of 2, the rapid early growth rate has slowed down and that boys are generally taller than girls. But this height difference has both advantages and disadvantages when it comes to developing movement and balance. For instance, smaller children can often run faster than tall children.

🧸🚚 **Toys:** ride-on toys with pedals, soft balls and bean bags for throwing and catching, outdoor garden play equipment

Stimulating Movement: 25 to 30 Months

Your child continues to increase in height and put on weight during her third year. And as a result of the continued process of physical, muscular and neurological maturation, she makes big progress in major movement skills such as jumping, running, climbing and balancing. Other children are of great interest to her now; when she sees them engaged in energetic, physical play she wants to get involved too.

I CAN'T DO IT

Your child's increased social awareness can have a negative effect on her self-esteem, in that her confidence may drop when she realizes some other children are more agile than she is. If she comes to you in tears claiming 'I can't run like my friend' take her feelings seriously. It may be a small matter to you but it's extremely important to your sensitive 2½-year-old. Give her a reassuring cuddle, comfort her until she calms down, tell her that she will improve as long as she continues to try hard, and remind her of all the other movement skills that she has already acquired.

Left: Now that your child's balance and coordination are good you can allow him more freedom in the playground – but he still needs watching at all times.

that her peers put direct pressure on her to do better – on the contrary, children this age rarely make comments about each others' physical ability. Rather, your child involuntarily compares herself with them,

Suitable Suggestions

You can encourage your toddler to become more active and more adventurous. You can show her how to move her body in ways that enhance her climbing and running skills. If you have a garden, some large outdoor play equipment is a great help. All of these strategies will sharpen her appetite for energetic play, but above all, make sure she spends plenty of time with other children her own age.

There is no bigger incentive to learn – for example, how to run faster – than the desire to keep up with a friend who races along at a furious pace. The same applies to all movement skills – watching others with different abilities boosts your child's determination to improve herself. It's not

Below: You can easily practise jumping with your child by holding his hands to help him balance as he pushes off the ground.

matching her skills against her friends' skills, and this fills her with a desire for self-improvement.

One of the best physical activities to improve your child's movement skills at this age is practice at jumping because this requires good balance, coordination of arm and leg movements, planning and muscular strength.

Above: When playing toddlers are constantly on the move, fetching, carrying, putting away, taking out, all of which help to refine their motor skills.

✤✤✤✤✤ Top ∙ Tips ✤✤✤✤✤

1. Make a small hurdle to jump over. Place a line of small wooden bricks a few centimetres in front of her feet. Ask her to jump over them. Even if she can't and she just hits them, she is unlikely to stumble.

2. Walk with her rather than pushing her in the buggy. Your journeys are generally slower when your child walks with you instead of being pushed along in a buggy, but she'll be getting much more practice with her movement skills.

3. Play tickling games with her. She enjoys being tickled by you, and she'll roll around the floor as you do this or she may run away in order for you to chase her. This is a fun way to exercise her movement skills.

4. Ask her to put her toys into the toy box. As well as giving your child a little bit of personal responsibility and independence, this regular task involves her in whole body movements, including walking, bending, balancing and placing.

5. Run alongside your child, holding her hand. She's not very steady on her feet but she'll make an attempt to move quicker when she has the security of knowing you're beside her to support her if she falls.

It's also one of those games that fills your child with pride when she manages to propel herself further or higher than she did on previous attempts.

You'll have noticed that when she was younger and she tried to jump into the air, she literally couldn't get her feet off the ground. She stood rooted to the spot, despite strenuous efforts, and looked at you in amazement wondering how you could manage to do it when she couldn't. This changes, however, during her third year. It all seems to come together as she succeeds in launching herself into the air and coming down again on the same spot. Initially, the gap between the soles of her feet and the floor is minimal, but over time this distance gradually increases.

Don't Forget Safety
If you don't already have them, you'll certainly need stairgates now at the top and bottom of the stairs in your house. However, your child's increasing agility means that she soon may be able to climb over them, so you still need to supervise her.

Q&A

Q Why is it that most boys seem to prefer strenuous outdoor play, while girls generally prefer to engage in more sedate activities?

A Nobody knows for sure why this difference occurs; some claim it is biological, while others say it is due to social expectations. Whatever the explanation, your child, whether a girl or a boy, should be encouraged to join in play activities involving balance, movement and coordination. Every child benefits from these games, irrespective of gender.

Q My child is afraid of climbing. Should I just put her on the climbing frame anyway?

A This will probably just terrify her further. Far better to encourage climbing ability slowly by starting with a small obstacle to climb, such as a cushion lying on the floor. Next, make the obstacle two cushions, gradually building up her confidence with more challenging feats. She'll tackle the climbing frame when she's ready.

Toys: soft cushioned play-mat, medium-sized football, garden slide with small ladder, pedal toy, music tapes and dance videos

Stimulating Movement: 31 to 36 Months

As your child reaches the end of his third year, he is more agile, tackles any obstacle in the playground and loves joining in energetic activities with his friends. He still gets into difficulties from time to time, however – so don't be surprised to hear him screaming when he gets all the way to the top of the climbing frame and then suddenly freezes, unable to descend alone.

Suitable Suggestions

Your child will have a go at anything involving movement now. Take running, for instance. Your 3-year-old dashes about furiously whenever the opportunity presents itself. You can help improve his speed, balance and coordination by setting up mini tracks for him to race around. Go into the garden and set out three small chairs about five metres apart, in a triangular formation. Suggest that your child runs around the chairs, until he arrives back at the first one.

He will manage to turn at the three corners without greatly slowing down his pace, as long as he concentrates on the task in hand.

When your child plays with a pedal toy, he can probably turn the pedals using his feet. Show your child how to place his soles on each pedal and then how to push so that the wheels turn. Initially, he will probably want to put his feet back on the ground, in order to propel himself along in the way that he's used to. But with your continued encouragement, and his perseverance, he'll eventually find that he can use pedal power to get the bike moving. And once he's made this discovery, there'll be no stopping him as he perfects the technique.

Try teaching him how to hop on one foot, though don't be surprised if this skill is beyond him at this stage. Hopping is a complex challenge, requiring good coordination between both sides of the brain, and your 3-year-old may simply not have the neurological maturation yet to achieve this. But there's no harm in trying it – he may just over-balance when he tries.

Left: Your child will feel very pleased with himself when he gets the hang of pedalling with his feet and steering at the same time.

Right: This little boy, at 34 months old, uses his outstretched arms to keep his balance as he stands on one leg.

Outdoor play is crucial for the development of your child's movement abilities. Of course there is plenty you can do with him indoors – there is no physical skill that can't be practised at home. Yet outdoor play on large, safe apparatus gives your child all the freedom he needs to experiment and to learn the extent of his agility. A small slide and ladder in the garden, along with perhaps a balancing log and a secure swing, provide endless hours of amusement for him. He'll have even more fun if you are able to take him to an adventure play area in the local park where he can also interact with other children.

Right: Your toddler will love being swung around by you. As long as you hold her firmly and make her feel secure, this sort of play can only enhance her physical skills.

✦✦✦✦✦✦ Top · Tips ✦✦✦✦✦✦

1. **Play movement games.** Have him face you and ask him to do what you do. Then do actions such as bending, lifting your leg, waving your arm, and so on. He'll make a good attempt to copy you.

2. **Use positive reinforcement.** He is more likely to succeed in pedalling his tricycle, for instance, if he knows you are waiting for him further along the path. Although he has built-in motivation, incentives such as a cuddle also help.

3. **Do 'pretend' marching.** Put on appropriate music, and then tell your child to follow you around the room, moving his arms and legs like you. He'll chuckle as he tries to coordinate his movements to simulate your marching style.

4. **Let him walk along a log.** He'll probably fall over, so you will need to hold his hand as he walks along it. This is a very difficult activity for your child, but a good way to encourage his balance and movement skills.

5. **Have fun with your child.** No matter what you do to enhance your child's movement skills, make sure that the activities remain fun. If you push him too hard, or if the games become too serious, he won't learn anything new.

Below: A low wall, log or beam provides excellent balancing practice; if your child wants to tackle these by himself then let him, as long as it is very low.

Q&A

Q Should I discourage rough-and-tumble play because it is quite aggressive?

A Rough-and-tumble play may look aggressive and destructive, but isn't. In fact, it's a very constructive form of play from a child's point of view because it develops his social and physical skills. If your child and his friends are happy playing this way – and it doesn't end in tears – leave them to get on with it.

Q I'm hopelessly uncoordinated and can't teach my child much in the way of movement. Will he lose out?

A Psychological research confirms that while parental interest in their child's movement skills has impact, children also learn about movement just from playing with others their own age. So do what you can to guide your child's physical activities and ensure that he has regular opportunities to spend time with his peers.

Toys: tricycle and other pedal toys, slide, climbing frame, see-saw, swingbouncer, balls for kicking and throwing

Hand-Eye

Coordination

The Importance of Hand–Eye Coordination

Although your toddler is more active, more mobile and more curious than ever before, she also needs to develop her hand–eye coordination to increase her learning and understanding. Between the ages of 15 months and 3 years, your child's hand control increases, enabling her to manipulate small objects, to gain better control over the use of cutlery and to fetch and carry items by herself.

Left: During this period your toddler will learn to manipulate smaller and more intricate toys.

Remember, too, that hand–eye control involves vision as well as finger movements. Your growing toddler has matured to the point where her vision and hand control combine effectively to enable her to focus keenly on a small toy that attracts her attention and then put her hand out to grab hold of it. Games that previously were too demanding for her, such as jigsaws, now hold great interest. The challenge of applying this new hand–eye coordination to solve even more difficult puzzles entices your determined toddler.

Hand Preference

Your child's hand preference – that is, whether she prefers to use her left or her right hand – was not noticeable at birth, but it will start to become apparent between the ages of 15 months and 3 years. You'll notice that she generally uses the same hand for most tasks involving manipulation. Research indicates that approximately one boy in ten and one girl in 12 is left-handed; over 90 per cent of children are obviously left-handed or right-handed by the time they reach school age.

Psychologists don't know for sure whether handedness is inborn or learned. There is a suggestion that a child who is right-handed may have broader brain connections to the right side of her body, which give her greater control over that side as compared to the left. However, there is also evidence that parents who are concerned about their infant's possible left-handedness and who gently encourage her to use her right hand, may succeed in creating a preference for the right. But this strategy only works with some children and is ineffective if started after the first year.

We live in a right-handed world. The majority of children use their right hand for opening doors, for cutting with scissors, for drawing, for handling small objects, and so on. Life is more difficult for left-handers – for example, learning to write is more challenging because a left-handed child tends to drag her hand over her writing or drawing, often smudging it.

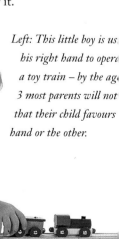

Left: This little boy is us[ing] his right hand to oper[ate] a toy train – by the ag[e] 3 most parents will not[e] that their child favours [one] hand or the other.

Don't be tempted to force your toddler to use her right hand if her natural preference seems to be to use the left hand. This could cause difficulties in other areas of development. For instance, there is some evidence that since hand preference is controlled by the part of the brain that also controls speech, forcing a left-handed toddler to use her right hand could create language difficulties. In addition, pressuring your toddler to go against her natural preference will result in confrontation and frustration and could create a problem where none existed before.

Drawing Skills

New opportunities for drawing emerge at this stage in your toddler's life. Until now, she assumed paper was something to be crumpled up and that a crayon was something to be chewed. Improved hand–eye coordination combined with more mature learning and understanding allows your child to begin the early stages of drawing. It doesn't matter if all she manages is to make a mark on the paper. Drawing adds an extra dimension to her life and is something you should encourage whenever your child shows an interest.

Aside from helping increase her hand–eye coordination skills even further – and giving her lots of fun – drawing brings your toddler plenty of other benefits. For instance, by enabling her to practise making different shapes and patterns, it increases her pattern-recognition skills, which are extremely important later on when it comes to learning to read. It can also have a very positive effect on her self-esteem. When she sees her drawings pinned up on the wall of your home, she is full of pride at her own achievements.

Drawing is also a good way for your growing toddler to express her feelings. You only need to watch her scribbling furiously at a piece of paper to know that she is totally involved in this activity. She can draw what she wants, use the crayon in any way that she wants, and can become as excited during this activity as she wants. It's a great form of emotional release.

Dealing with Frustration

You'll know from your own experience of, say, trying to thread a needle or attempting to sew on a button, that activities involving hand–eye coordination can be very

Above: At 2 years old this toddler knows how to remove the jar lid but does not yet have the coordination or strength to do it.

frustrating when they don't go according to plan. Your toddler feels the same way when that annoying last piece of the jigsaw won't fit or when the lid infuriatingly holds firmly on to the box despite all her efforts to dislodge it. Calm your frustrated toddler, and then show her how to complete the activity in a methodical, relaxed manner.

Below: This 18-month-old's inability to manoeuvre his blanket in the way he would like is leading to frustration. This can be a common emotion at this stage in a toddler's development.

Hand–Eye Coordination

Age	Skill

15–18 months
Your toddler's hand control has extended significantly, and he is probably able to hold two items in each hand at the same time.

He sees the connection between his hand movements and the immediate environment and recognizes that he has some control over his actions.

He loves making marks on paper, whether using crayons or paints, and will happily fill sheet after sheet.

19–21 months
He thoroughly enjoys playing games with balls, both large and small, and attempts to roll them, throw them and even catch them.

He is able to stack small wooden blocks on top of each other to make a tall tower without it falling over.

Your toddler loves water play and is able to pour water from one container into another one without much spilling.

22–24 months
He takes great pleasure from looking at books with you and will be content to sit for several minutes studying each picture and turning the pages.

His increased hand–eye coordination makes him want to help get himself dressed and undressed. The more you encourage him, the more adept he'll become.

From 15 Months to 3 Years

What to Do

Place your child in a comfortable, upright sitting position. Take a couple of quite small toys and put them in his left hand. Immediately put another two in his right hand – he'll hold all four in his hands for a few seconds.

Sit your toddler on the floor with a small towel spread out in front of him so that one corner is near his hand. Put a small toy on the other corner of the towel and ask him to get it – you'll find that he pulls at the corner of the towel nearest to his hand in order to bring the toy towards him.

Make sure he has easy access to plenty of paper and crayons (the chubby sort that are easy for small hands to grasp) so that he can draw whenever he wants. You could also let him do finger painting – this can be a very messy activity but he'll love it. Let him see that you are interested in the results.

Your toddler can be either seated or standing during this activity. Put a medium-sized, light plastic ball in his hands – so that he holds it firmly in front of him – and ask him to throw the ball. He will try to do this although the ball may go in any direction.

Seat your toddler at a table. Place some small wooden blocks nearby and ask him to make a tower. (Demonstrate this if he is at all unsure.) With a little practice, he'll be able to build a tower with five or more bricks before it topples over.

Give your toddler one empty plastic cup and another half full of water. Ask him to pour the water from the half-full cup into the empty one. He will probably be able to manage this without spilling.

Choose a children's book with robust pages that will withstand the rough handling of a young child. Either sit beside your toddler or place him on your lap. Let him hold the book. Then look at the pictures on each page. He'll point to the ones that he recognizes.

When bathtime approaches, tell your 2-year-old that you would like him to help you with undressing. He won't manage zip fastenings, but he'll probably be able partly to remove some items himself, such as socks and possibly a loose-fitting jumper.

Hand–Eye Coordination

Age	Skill

He has a well-controlled pincer grip – in other words, he can coordinate index finger and thumb effectively to pick up small objects.

25–30 months

Bead-threading is an activity that may attract his interest since it gives him the opportunity to practise his improving hand–eye coordination.

His confidence has grown and he is now able to manage many more tasks that require good hand control, such as painting and drawing.

He is able to cope with construction toys and games that involve different pieces that have to be placed together in a specific way before they connect.

31–36 months

He begins to be able to cut paper with a pair of scissors, though he may find this difficult. He needs your encouragement – without it he may give up too easily.

His pencil control has improved and his drawing is less random. You can usually see what his pictures are supposed to represent.

Your child likes to help you around the house, sometimes simply copying whatever you do and sometimes actually carrying out a practical task for you.

From 15 Months to 3 Years

What to Do

Place a small toy in front of him and ask him to pick it up. Whereas at a younger age he would have tried to sweep it up in the palm of his hand, he now tries to use his thumb and index finger. He does this slowly, and may become agitated if it slips from his grasp.

Buy a set of large wooden beads and some laces. (Keep an eye on him while he plays with the beads just in case he thinks it is a good idea to taste them!) Your child will soon master how to thread the lace through the hole.

When given a crayon and paper, you'll notice that he grips the crayon in his hand more maturely. Instead of grasping it in the palm of his hand, he holds it firmly with three or four fingers and has no difficulty making a deliberate mark on the paper.

Let him play with various types of interlocking plastic bricks – he has endless fun making different shapes. In addition, ask him to build a tower with small wooden blocks. At this age, he can build a steady tower perhaps seven or eight blocks high.

Buy a pair of child-safe scissors, with handles for small hands and with protective covers on the edges of the blades to minimize risk of injury. With practice and support, your child will learn to grip the scissors properly and use them to cut through a piece of paper.

As well as letting him do free drawing, suggest that he draws certain shapes. For instance, draw a circle on a piece of paper and then ask him to do the same – he tries hard to copy the design, although the ends of the circle might not meet.

Use his interest in housework to consolidate his hand–eye coordination. For example, his hand control is good enough for him to dust a table-top, to put toys back into the toy box, and even to put cutlery on the table before meals.

Stimulating Hand–Eye Coordination: 15 to 18 Months

Your toddler is able to do much more for herself. She can strut about, going wherever the mood takes her – and that means her little hands explore all those places you'd prefer to be left alone, such as electric sockets, flaps in video recorders, and inside cupboards. You'll need to keep a watchful eye on her at all times.

Right: Finger painting is a wonderful way to encourage your child to use her fingers and she will have great fun.

BALANCING SAFETY WITH CHALLENGE

Now that she feels more confident about her hand control, your toddler enjoys manipulating small objects. Therefore zips, tiny buttons, pins lying on the floor, small wooden beads, bits of dried food that she discovers, all fascinate her. She wants to pick them up and explore them, and perhaps even put them in her mouth.

She needs this sort of hands-on experience to develop her hand–eye coordination even further, but there is a risk of injury if she is unsupervised. You have to balance your safety concerns with her need for varied play opportunities. So keep all sharp items out of reach and watch over her very carefully when she plays with permitted small items.

Suitable Suggestions

Give her a wooden puzzle (called an inset board) that has different shapes cut out, which your child then has to fit back into the correct empty spaces on the board. She will enjoy spending time on these, but do remember that they are extremely difficult for her and she may become frustrated when the pieces don't fit the way she wants. Stick to inset boards that have basic, brightly coloured shapes, such as circles, triangles and squares. Those with irregular shapes are probably too demanding for her at this age.

Make sure she has plenty of paper and crayons close to hand. Drawing is one of those activities that she never tires of because she is

able to create something new every time. Encourage your toddler to sit at a small table while drawing so that she is comfortable and relaxed. You won't be able to decipher her drawings at this stage, even though she may insist that she has drawn, for example, you or your house. Don't criticize her sketches, otherwise she will very quickly lose interest in drawing.

Left: By now your toddler is gaining a good understanding of what different tools and utensils are for and enjoys playing with toy versions.

Left: Let your child help to dress and undress himself – even if he does need some assistance.

At this age, she may like to get involved with dressing and undressing. For instance, as you approach with her jumper, she may stick her hands and arms towards you in anticipation. Or she may try to pull her socks off her feet. Bear in mind that your toddler's ambitions outstrip her ability – so you may discover her in tears one day, with her jumper stuck half-way over her head, as she tries unsuccessfully to wrestle the item off completely. Show your approval when she does try to help in this way, but reassure and support her as necessary.

The same applies with feeding, whether snacks or meals. Her determination to do things by herself means that at mealtimes she insists on using the spoon to feed herself. Her hand control is not fully developed yet and therefore some of the food lands on the floor or on the table. Be prepared for a certain amount of mess and let her practise every day.

Above: Simple inset boards with pegged pieces are suitable for this age group though you may need to be on hand to help.

✦✦✦✦✦✦✦ Top·Tips ✦✦✦✦✦✦✦

1. Keep her calm. If your child becomes tearful when, for instance, she can't lift the small piece of food from her plate, first calm her. Her hand–eye control diminishes when she's upset. When she is calm, encourage her to try again, but perhaps more slowly this time.

2. Make a special display area for her drawings. There is no better way to express your admiration of her drawing skills than by displaying her work prominently. You could set aside an area of the kitchen wall solely for this purpose.

3. Don't force hand preference. By now she probably prefers to use the same hand consistently for tasks involving hand–eye control. Let this aspect develop naturally. Certainly, never force a left-handed child to use her right hand instead.

4. Roll a ball back and forth. Sit a few metres away from your child, on the floor, and roll a ball towards her – when she has caught it firmly, ask her to roll it back to you. Although you find this easy, it's a challenge for her, so be patient.

5. Play clapping games. By now she is able to clap her hands together, but you can encourage her to clap less randomly. For instance, clap your hands together once and then again a second later. Ask her to copy you. Clapping along with music is also good practice.

Q My toddler doesn't seem to understand how cause-and-effect toys work. What should I do to encourage her?

A It may be that her hand–eye coordination simply isn't good enough yet to operate the toys you give her. Check that they have been designed for her age group. If she doesn't understand how to make a toy work, then just show her what to do with it. You may need to do this a few times.

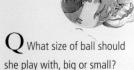

Q What size of ball should she play with, big or small?

A She needs a range of sizes. Different sizes require her to use different visual and manual skills. A small ball helps her strengthen her grip because she can hold it in one hand alone. A larger ball requires her to coordinate both hands in order to grasp the ball.

Toys: inset board with chunky handles, small soft balls of different sizes, building blocks that lock together

Stimulating Hand–Eye Coordination: 19 to 21 Months

His improved attention span enables your child to cope with more complex hand–eye coordination challenges. At times he is totally preoccupied with, say, lifting something from a plate or fitting a toy together – his face is a picture of concentration as he persists in his attempt to complete the activity. Your toddler's increased confidence motivates him to try harder with more difficult games and puzzles.

PRACTICE MAKES PERFECT

The typical toddler this age likes to get things right first time. And if he doesn't, temper and tears may follow. This often shows through with activities involving hand–eye coordination because they need concentration and patience to achieve steady hand movements. When the piece of the inset board doesn't immediately fit, he may end up hurling it across the room.

Encourage your toddler to practise again and again with any hand–eye coordination task that he finds particularly difficult. Explain to him that everyone learns gradually and that the more he tries, the easier it will become.

Left: By 18 months most children are able to build a small tower with bricks and will enjoy playing with building blocks.

and puzzles – he may prefer familiarity to novelty. Once you are aware of his level of hand–eye coordination, buy him an inset board that is difficult for him to complete but not too demanding. If he puts it to one side at first, sit with him and suggest that you do it together.

Your toddler finds it easier to concentrate on a hand–eye coordination activity when there are few other visual distractions. Suggest that he clears some of his other toys away before starting on something new. Having

Suitable Suggestions

He will naturally tend to play with toys that he can manage without too much difficulty. For instance, he'll play with inset boards he has already mastered, even though they are no longer a challenge. You may need to encourage him to persist with new toys

Right: Your toddler will watch everything you do and can copy quite sophisticated actions.

only one toy at a time in his immediate visual field increases the likelihood that he'll complete the task. Give him lots of praise when he does persist until completion.

He does lots of reaching and touching, whether or not you give him permission. This is a sign of natural curiosity, not naughtiness, and is probably best dealt with in a firm but relaxed manner. Tell him what he can and cannot touch around the house, and explain why not. Your toddler is now at the age where he begins to understand explanations. The same applies when you visit someone else's house – tell him

Above: Toddlers at this age are ready to start exploring different textures like sand and water.

beforehand that he mustn't touch objects in the house and remind him again as necessary when you are there. Be prepared for him to try to bend the rules, however. You will need to remain vigilant for potential hazards.

If you can, provide access to a sand-and-water tray. Mix the sand with just enough cold water to create a firm texture – if you make it too runny, there's not much he can do with it. Getting his hands messy in this play mixture is good for his hand–eye coordination. He can squeeze the sand mud between his fingers, build shapes with it or even draw pictures in its smooth surface.

Below: Play doh or clay will help develop good hand–eye coordination and engage your child's imagination.

Q & A

Q Why does my toddler's hand often tremble when he concentrates on putting shapes into the correct holes?

A This is a normal occurrence during an activity requiring great concentration. His desire to fit the shape in the hole is so strong that his hand and arm muscles start to tense up, and his whole hand begins to shake. It stops shaking when he relaxes.

Q My toddler won't let me help him when he struggles with undressing. What should I do?

A Although he won't let you give him a hand, you can still talk to him and can give helpful directions (for instance, 'Pull that sock off first, not both at once'). Once he starts to listen to your comments, he'll be more willing to let you give practical help.

Toys: set of stacking rings or beakers, doll with buttons and zips on its clothing, construction blocks of varying shapes and sizes

✦✦✦✦✦✦✦ Top · Tips ✦✦✦✦✦✦✦

1. Resist the temptation to compare your child. He will develop hand–eye coordination at his own rate. You may know other children his age who have better hand control than he does, but comparisons with them only make you anxious and dent his self-confidence.

2. Provide modelling materials. He can make any shape he wants from clay or play doh, and if he doesn't like what he has made, he can squash it and start again. As long as it doesn't dry out, clay or doh can be used again and again.

3. Wiggle his fingers. Demonstrate how you can stretch your hands wide open and wiggle your fingers in the air. Your toddler will try to imitate you, although he'll find that he can't move his fingers in such a coordinated fashion as you.

4. Play 'pointing' games. Name specific objects in the room and ask your child to point to them. He'll then scan the area, spot the object you have named and point his index finger towards it. This type of 'I spy' game is great fun.

5. Use household items. His hand–eye control benefits when he plays with everyday items. Dried pasta, for instance, can be arranged into many different patterns, and flour and water combine into a sticky mixture that he can manipulate.

Stimulating Hand–Eye Coordination: 22 to 24 Months

As she approaches the end of her second year, your toddler's fascination with other children her own age is strong. Although she does not yet play cooperatively, she watches her peers closely and will try to imitate their style of play. This can act as an incentive for her to play with toys and games that she was not particularly interested in before.

STEP BY STEP

When faced with a challenge involving hand–eye coordination, your toddler might feel overwhelmed – she thinks it is simply too much for her. You can help her develop hand control by teaching her how to approach the activity in small steps. Suppose, for instance, she struggles to fit shapes into a shape sorter. Show her a strategy. Explain that she should select one shape only, and that she should then take that shape to the first hole to see if it fits. If it doesn't, she should move the same shape to the next hole, and then repeat the process until she achieves success.

Suitable Suggestions

Whenever possible, arrange for your child to play with others her own age – she learns from and is motivated by their actions. For instance, if she sees another 2-year-old playing with construction blocks, she'll probably want to do the same herself, even if she isn't interested in these toys when she is on her own. The attraction of the example of her peers encourages her to develop new hand–eye coordination skills. Her social development, however, still has a long way to go and she may simply grab a toy from another child instead of asking for it.

This is a good time to develop her ability to pass and receive objects from hand to hand. Her hand control is

Above: Passing an object to someone else and from hand to hand is something he can now achieve.

sufficiently established for her to be able to pick up an item, pass it to you and let go once you have taken hold of it. She can also do this action in reverse. Practise this with, say, a plastic cup or a small toy. Initially it might slip from her grasp at the change-over stage, but her skill will steadily improve.

Right: Children of this age don't often play cooperatively but will unconsciously absorb new skills by watching and copying each other.

Above: Your child's use of instruments will be less random and more controlled though it may not sound it!

Your toddler is beginning to enjoy musical instruments. Whereas before she would have struggled to beat a plastic drumstick against a toy drum or to shake a tambourine in a coordinated way, her improved hand control allows her to make more planned use of toy musical instruments. Give her a range of these toys and let her play freely with them to discover their possibilities. Encourage her to use them as she listens to music. She will have great fun listening to the 'music' that she, in turn, creates.

Once she is comfortable with the instruments, ask her to beat the drum as you sing her a song. Show her how to grasp the stick at the end, holding it firmly in her hand, and start the song. Her beats on the drum will probably be random rather than rhythmical at first, but her skill will improve with practice. You could help her by moving your hand up and down every time she is to beat the drum. Be patient – moving her hand in time to music is difficult and she won't achieve mastery of this skill properly until much later.

Below: Giving your child some choice over what he wears will make him more enthusiastic about dressing himself.

✦✦✦✦✦✦✦ Top·Tips ✦✦✦✦✦✦✦

1. Allow her to choose some of her clothes. She'll be more enthusiastic about trying to dress and undress herself if she has chosen the items to wear. Help her make the choice if she is unsure to start with.

2. Encourage her to clear up. For instance, once she has finished her meal, she can lift her plate and cutlery and carry it to the sink. Remind her that it's easier to carry only one item at a time.

3. Give her colouring books to play with. She won't be able to keep the crayon marks within the outlines yet, but this provides good early practice for writing skills. You'll find that at this stage she just scribbles in broad, sweeping movements.

4. Let her open doors. If she is tall enough to reach the door handle, show her how to turn it and then to pull the door open. Supervise her at first, as opening the door might knock her off-balance.

5. Give her a toy telephone with an old-fashioned dial. To turn the dial effectively, your toddler has to insert one finger in a hole and then rotate her whole hand slowly. This requires good hand–eye coordination and plenty of patience.

Q My child won't give up when she can't finish a jigsaw, even when she gets upset. What should I do?

A Suggest she temporarily leaves the challenge that upsets her and then returns to it later once she is calm. When you see her struggling, distract her with another activity – perhaps give her a drink of juice – and then let her go back to the activity.

Q Why does my toddler often fall over when she bends down to pick something up from the floor with her pincer grip?

A Picking something off the floor involves both hand–eye coordination and balance at the same time, and this may be too demanding for her. Putting all her concentration into coordinating her thumb and forefinger reduces her focus on balance – and hence she topples.

🧸🚂 **Toys:** toy musical instruments, jigsaw puzzles, peg board with large pegs, nesting barrels that screw together

Stimulating Hand–Eye Coordination: 25 to 30 Months

Your child is developing a more defined sense of self; in other words, he has a clearer understanding of his abilities, of what he can and cannot do, and he chooses to use his talents in ways that he sees fit. Improved hand–eye coordination, for example, enables him to be more independent, to pick up and manipulate objects without having to ask you for help. He thoroughly enjoys this increasing freedom.

THE UNACCEPTABLE SIDE OF HAND CONTROL

When roused to anger, your child is tempted to hit the source of his irritation – whether that is his brother, sister or parent. Without thinking through his action, he impulsively raises his hand and whacks the object of his wrath. Such misuse of his hand control skills is totally unacceptable and should always be discouraged.

Make sure your child understands that you are angry at his aggressive action, explain that he should express his displeasure verbally not physically, and ask him to consider what he would feel like if someone hit him in that way. You will probably have to repeat this process again and again until he gains better control of his impulses.

Suitable Suggestions

Your toddler occasionally tries to impose his ideas on other people within the family, whether they like it or not. For instance, if he wants you to read him a book, he looks for it, finds it, brings it over to you and puts it on your lap; if he thinks that it is time for something special to eat, then he goes to the cupboard, selects the item and brings it to you. However, his increased assertiveness stems from his developing skills, not from any underlying character trait. But you'll probably need to be assertive yourself, in order to ensure that he doesn't end up in charge!

Above: By now your child's manual skills will be improving all the time and you will notice how much better he is at puzzles and building towers.

Invite him to open packages for you. This could be a paper bag containing a food item, or a wrapped parcel, or a screw-top jar. His hand–eye coordination is developed enough for him to be able to cope with many of these manual challenges. Use events that arise in your daily routine, such as getting a slice of bread from the packet or opening the breakfast cereal box. If it proves too much for your child, half open the packet for him and leave him to complete the job.

Left: Children over 2 will have the dexterity to open boxes, wrapped parcels and containers that have screw-on lids.

Above: Drawing is now more controlled and your child will be able to copy simple shapes.

✦✦✦✦✦✦ Top · Tips ✦✦✦✦✦✦

1. Teach him baking. He delights in mixing dough, rolling it out on the table and cutting it into small shapes. Watch his face when he sees his own 'biscuits' brought fully baked from the oven. He wants the whole family to taste them.

2. Show him how to use cutlery. He already uses a spoon but try to teach him how to use cutlery in each hand. Start with a fork in one hand and a spoon in the other. This takes time to master.

3. Give him varied drawing and painting equipment. Buy a range of coloured pencils, crayons and types of paper so that your child has choices when it comes to creative activities. Encourage him to vary the materials he selects.

4. Praise his independence. Each new stage of independence brings him pride and boosts his self-confidence, especially when he knows you are pleased with him. So, for example, give him a big cuddle when he manages to dress himself more or less properly.

5. Buy him a toy tool set. As well as developing imaginative play, he will improve his hand control by pretend-playing with plastic tools. Actions such as sawing, hammering and turning a screwdriver all provide excellent practice.

Practise fastening buttons with him. Instead of using his clothes, take a small square of cloth and sew three large buttons on to it, spaced at least two centimetres apart. Take another piece of cloth and cut three large buttonholes in it, matching them exactly to the spacing of the buttons on the other piece of cloth. Now you have all the equipment needed for your child to improve his buttoning skills. At first, he should try to complete only one button at a time, but once he has mastered this, suggest he fastens two buttons to the top cloth and then three.

Your child's maturing drawing skills mean that he is more able to copy shapes accurately. While he watches you, draw a vertical line on a piece of blank paper and tell him to 'draw one just like that'. His line will be shaky but it will be clear and in the correct orientation.

Below: Cooking is an opportunity for your child to practise a range of manual skills and making something will give her a great sense of achievement.

Q My child is 30 months old and obsessed with dressing and undressing dolls. Is that normal?

A Yes. Children this age often become fixated with one toy in particular. Yours has turned his attention to playing with dolls like this because his hand control has developed to the point where he achieves success every time. Encourage him to play with other toys too.

Q How many pieces should a 2½-year-old be able to replace in an inset board?

A As a rough guide, you could expect a child of this age to cope with a board that has three or four different pieces. The difficulty of an inset board is also affected by the shape of the inserts – irregular, large shapes are harder to fit than small regular shapes.

Toys: threading beads and laces, boxes with lids, construction bricks, jigsaws, toy cars, finger puppets

Stimulating Hand–Eye Coordination: 31 to 36 Months

As she approaches the end of her third year, your child's hand control is becoming very sophisticated. So many of the activities that were previously beyond her are now well within her abilities. For instance, her cup-holding skill, her use of cutlery, her effectiveness at picking up and carrying objects, and her competence at dressing herself all help to make her much more self-reliant.

FROM INSET BOARDS TO JIGSAWS

Your child is ready to move from inset board puzzles to jigsaw puzzles at this age, though the transition is challenging. Unlike inset boards, jigsaw puzzles have no outer frame to guide your child. Pieces can fit anywhere in any orientation, so there are more possible combinations than for the pieces of an inset board.

Initially, buy your child a two-piece jigsaw only, one that has an easily identifiable picture. The picture, rather than the shapes of the pieces, will guide her. Once she has achieved a two-piece jigsaw, progress to a three-piece then a four-piece, and so on. Build up the degree of difficulty gradually.

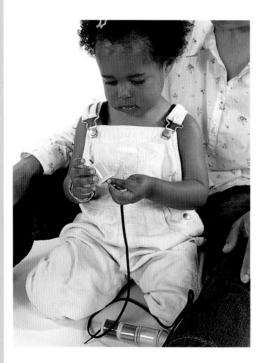

Suitable Suggestions

Your child's hand–eye coordination has reached the point where she is able to undertake ever more varied and interesting craft activities. She loves cutting up bits of paper with scissors – although this remains difficult for her – and then sticking these small pieces on to a larger sheet of paper in a random pattern. Use paper glue that is

Right: Cutting and sticking can still be quite a challenge but is great fun.

Left: This 32-month-old girl is completely absorbed as she threads bobbins on a piece of cord.

suitable for children (obtainable from toy shops) and be prepared for a bit of a mess.

You'll need to guide her until she becomes more skilled at using scissors. Cutting is a complex hand control task that takes a long time to achieve, so your child needs your encouragement. Never let her use ordinary scissors because they are not safe for small hands. Buy her safety scissors designed for children from a good toy shop.

Her drawings are also becoming more interesting. Your child has probably

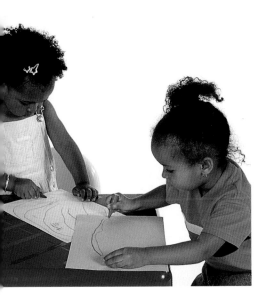

Left: At this age children begin to draw people or objects they see around them and elements of these drawings will start to be recognizable.

always enjoyed drawing pictures of people, but they have hardly been recognizable. They are becoming more accurate and you can tell the subject. You'll notice the head of the person in the drawing is disproportionately large, and the legs are like little sticks jutting out from the underside; 3-year-olds generally miss out the body altogether. There are usually no other details, except perhaps a couple of pencil points to represent the eyes.

Motivate your child to use her hand–eye coordination purposefully to improve her daily life. For instance, she is probably reliably clean and dry during the day. With her level of hand control, she should be able to dress and undress herself for the toilet – she's thrilled when you point out to her that she is like 'a big girl' now. This is also a good time to teach her how to wash her hands after using the toilet. The taps may be too difficult for her to turn but encourage her to try anyway. Show her how to rub her hands together under the running water and dry them on the towel.

Below: Nearing 3 years old, your child will get great stimulation from meeting other children and playing with different toys at play group or nursery.

✥✥✥✥✥✥✥ Top · Tips ✥✥✥✥✥✥✥

1. Give her time. Now that she attempts more complex hand–eye coordination games and activities, she needs lots of time to relax and concentrate on them. Let her continue until she achieves her goal, and resist the temptation to hurry her along.

2. Plan outings. It takes longer for your child to use the toilet without help from you than with your help. This can be frustrating for you when you are in a rush to go out. Don't undermine her confidence by hurrying her, but ask her to use the toilet well before you intend to leave on your trip.

3. Encourage more accurate colouring. Point out to your child how her crayon marks go over the black outlines. Suggest that she tries a little bit harder to keep the crayons closer to the lines themselves, by making slower hand movements.

4. Allocate responsibility. She'll love involvement in your household routine, such as being responsible for dusting a table top, or for sweeping a rug with a small brush. Her hand control means that she can complete these jobs if she tries.

5. Take her to nursery or playgroup. She will benefit from mixing with other children, from playing with them in novel ways, and from having access to a new range of toys.

Q&A

Q My 3-year-old has good hand control but prefers me to fetch and carry for her. How can I change this?

A Resist carrying out tasks you know she is capable of doing. Eventually her desire for the toy or the piece of food will become so strong that she will get it herself. And when she does, reinforce her behaviour by telling her how delighted you are that she did this all by herself.

Q How many wooden blocks should a child of this age be able to stack to make a tower?

A Most 3-year-olds can build a tower of nine or ten blocks. Yet an uneven table leg or a slippery table top can easily make the tower fall before it reaches that height. Don't worry if she only manages, say, seven or eight blocks in the tower.

🧸🚂 **Toys:** plastic tea set, art and craft materials, toy farm animals, toy figures, plastic or wooden train set with tracks

Language

The Progress of Language

If you gasped in amazement at your baby's language development during the first year – when he changed from a baby who could only cry into someone who could say his first clear word – then you will be stunned by the language explosion that occurs when he is a toddler! In his second and third years, his language takes a tremendous surge forward, enabling him to take part in conversations, to relate his experiences and to voice his feelings.

Here are some of the main changes to look for:

• **vocabulary.** At the age of 15 months, he can probably use about six clear words, most of which are names of people in the family or familiar objects. Estimates vary but it is safe to assume that by the time he is 3 years old, he can use more than a thousand words, and of course he understands a lot more. His vocabulary is very varied by this stage, and he is able to use words in an appropriate context in order to communicate effectively.

• **structure.** His ability to combine words together to form phrases and short sentences develops. Initially, he could say only one word at a time, each word representing a complete thought. But around the age of 18 months, he starts to combine two words together to form a meaningful phrase, such as

'me teddy', meaning 'I want my teddy', and by the age of 3 he talks in short structured sentences, with at least three or four words in them.

• **grammar.** The typical 3-year-old uses different types of words, not just nouns as he did when he first began to speak, but also adjectives, verbs and pronouns. For instance, he might say 'I want my teddy', clearing indicating his wishes in a grammatically correct sentence. He starts using words such as 'in' and 'on', and he is able to add 's' on to a word sometimes to make it plural. (In some cases he may do this incorrectly, for example, saying 'mouses' instead of 'mice'.) However, it's not until much later that he learns to use present, past and future tenses.

• **pronunciation.** Your toddler uses most consonants and vowels, although at times he becomes

confused. Word beginnings in particular often get mixed (for example, 'lellow' instead of 'yellow'). You may be tempted to laugh when he makes these normal mistakes but do your best not to. In any case, his speech is clear enough for most other children and adults to understand.

Listening Skills

Your child becomes a better listener during his second and third years, which aids his language development because it is through listening that he hears language spoken, and this enables him to interpret instructions and take part in conversations. Remember, however, that he remains egocentric

Below: At 30 months old this little boy's vocabulary is wide and he is able to name the different parts of the body.

Above: At 3 years old your child will be able to make himself understood to other children and adults, most of the time.

– he still expects the world to revolve around him and therefore he will often not feel any need to listen to you when you talk to him.

When you find that, for instance, your 3-year-old continues to watch television after you have asked him to come to the dining table for his evening meal, the chances are that he heard you but deliberately chose to ignore your message. At this age, he's good at exercising 'selective attention'! On the other hand, a child who consistently fails to respond to comments directed at him may have a hearing problem.

If you're not sure whether your child ignores you by choice or because he simply doesn't hear properly, look for other possible indications of hearing impairment. For instance, he might study your face and mouth closely when you speak, he might ask you to repeat questions over and over, or he might mix up certain sounds in his speech (such as 't' and 'k'). None of these findings definitely signify a hearing loss, but if you are at all concerned, have his hearing checked by your family doctor.

Why Speak?

Your child's ability to talk not only enables him to express himself easily and accurately, but also allows him to gather information – it's a great means of satisfying his endless curiosity. That's why your 2- or 3-year-old starts to ask questions, and once he starts, he doesn't stop!

Prepare yourself for an onslaught of 'why', 'who', 'how', and 'what' questions. He doesn't ask these questions in order to confront you or to challenge your views; he has a genuine interest in the replies. You'll discover that he has an amazing ability to ask about things that leave you at a loss for any easy answer. For instance, 'Why is the

car that colour?' or 'Why do you have hair?'

He is also likely to repeat questions, even though you thought you had answered them already. The fact is that your child may not have understood your initial explanation and so he wants you to tell him again. This can be exceedingly frustrating for you, but his question

Above: From the age of 2 onwards children ask increasing numbers of questions as they try to understand the world around them.

stems from a genuine desire to use his improved language skills to enhance his understanding of the world around him. He may use endless questions as a way of gaining and keeping your attention, which he loves. He'll have already learned that when you are talking to him, no matter what the subject matter, you are focused on him – and he wants to keep it that way.

Left: As she comprehends more, she will become more attentive and conversations will be less simplistic.

Language

Age	Skill
15–18 months	Your toddler is able to use approximately six or seven different, identifiable words, and she uses them consistently. She understands many more words than that, of course. Her language is often a mixture of real words and 'jabber', and she may have her own words for people or objects, which she uses consistently.
	She is able to listen to instructions, interpret them accurately and then carry out the request, as long as the instructions carry only one piece of information in them.
	She effectively combines aspects of both verbal and non-verbal communication in order to express her basic needs and desires to you; she will persist until you show her that you understand.
19–21 months	She still uses single words but now they are often put together to form a short two-word phrase. Each phrase has its own meaning, and is used appropriately by her.
	Your child loves spotting familiar objects in picture books, as long as there are not too many objects on the page, and also identifying familiar people in family photographs.
	Conversations interest your child. She no longer says what she thinks the moment it enters her head, but instead is ready to listen and to wait for a gap before speaking.
22–24 months	Your child's awareness of herself as an individual gradually increases at this age and she can now can reliably name the main parts of her body.
	As a result partly of her increased vocabulary and partly of her increased understanding, your 2-year-old can name a set of everyday objects that are placed in front of her.

From 15 Months to 3 Years

What to Do

Make a note of all the words she uses over a three-day period. You may find that sometimes she jabbers without appearing to use any recognizable words, but in most instances she reliably uses the same word to indicate the same object each time.

Ask your toddler to complete an activity that you know is well within her capability, for instance, 'Pass me the cup'. If she is in a responsive mood, she understands what you say and fulfils your request. She does this even though she can't say the words herself.

Instead of trying to anticipate her request, wait for her to say it to you. If there is something that your child specifically wants – for instance, for you to switch on the television – she will point to it and say the word simultaneously. Give her plenty of time to find the words she needs.

Help her combine words by replying with a phrase when she uses a single word. For instance, when she asks 'Daddy?', you can say 'Where's Daddy?' and then reply. Let her know how pleased you are when she forms phrases like this.

Sit your child on your knee or beside you and let her turn over the pages of her favourite picture book. She points out all the different people, animals and objects and tries to name them. If she hasn't told you the word for the picture after a few seconds, tell her what it is.

Chat to your child about the toys she is playing with, then look at her while pausing for her to respond verbally. You'll find that her ability to time her comments to respond to yours increases around this age, and she is more prepared to take turns while talking.

Say to her 'Show me your feet' and wait for her to point to them. Do the same for her eyes, ears, nose, mouth and hands. You'll find that she knows most of these, and with your help she'll learn the rest over the next few months.

Set out around six familiar objects on a tray – for example, a pencil, a ball, a cup, a teddy, a spoon and a book. Bring the tray over to your child, point to one of the objects and ask her 'What's that?' She can probably name most of them.

Language

Age	Skill
	She will probably be becoming more interested in what others are saying, and will silently listen to conversations even though she is not being addressed directly.
25–30 months	She loves you reading stories to her just before she goes to sleep. It's not just the intimacy of the story-telling process that she likes but also the content of the story itself.

Her understanding of spoken language has developed considerably. She is able to ask a question, listen attentively to the answer and then make sense of what was said to her.

Her memory has improved to the extent that she can recall small amounts of personal information and can reliably relay it to a familiar child or adult.

31–36 months   Pronouns such as 'I' and 'me' start to feature regularly in her speech. She doesn't always use them properly, often using 'me' instead of 'I'.

By now her vocabulary has extended to at least a thousand words that she can use both confidently and appropriately.

She begins to understand the basic grammar of language and that it follows rules. She can't actually explain what these rules are but she can usually apply them.

From 15 Months to 3 Years

What to Do

At times, encourage your toddler to stay beside you when you chat to a friend. Of course, she'll eventually lose interest and want to play on her own, but while she's listening she'll be extending her language skills.

Tuck her up in bed at night, and then sit on the bed beside her and read her a story. Make sure you pick one that isn't too scary and that doesn't get her too excited. She relaxes as she listens to you, so this is good preparation for her to fall asleep.

When she asks you a question, position yourself so that you are face-to-face with her when you reply. Do your best to keep her attention if she starts to become distracted by something else in the room. Ask her to repeat what you told her.

Encourage your child to respond to simple questions about herself from friends and members of the family – for example, telling them her name and age. However, there may be times when your child is so overcome with shyness that she can't manage this. Don't pressurize her to speak if she is embarrassed by the situation.

Demonstrate the correct form of speech, without criticizing her wording. For instance, when she announces to you that 'me want juice now', you could respond by saying 'I would like some juice, too.' This gives a good example of language for her to copy.

Spend some time just observing your child and listening to her when she plays with her friends or talks to her siblings. You'll probably be surprised at the wide range of words she uses that she has learned from a rich variety of sources in her life.

Make one hand into a funny shape and tell her you have called it, for example, a 'pid'. Then make both hands the same shape and say 'Here are two….' She'll probably reply 'pids', proving she understands the rule of adding an 's' to a word to make it plural.

Stimulating Language: 15 to 18 Months

Your toddler's vocabulary starts to build steadily as he listens to conversations around him. Typically he uses several different words a day – and understands the meaning of literally hundreds more – and he begins to form meaningful two-word phrases. You quickly discover that there is one word that he likes to use himself and yet hates anyone else to use, and that's 'no'!

READ TO YOUR TODDLER

Reading to your toddler is one of the great contributions you can make to his speech development. Even though he may seem to listen passively as you go through the story, studies have found that young children who listen to stories read to them by their parent for just 10 or 15 minutes each day usually have more advanced language development than those children who miss out on this valuable experience.

Of course, your toddler can also improve his speech skills by listening to other sources of stimulation, such as television and video tapes, but there is something very special about you reading to him, something that harnesses his imagination and enthusiasm more than most other forms of language stimulation.

Suitable Suggestions

It's important to make good eye contact when chatting to your child. As well as grabbing his attention and improving his listening skills, encouraging him to maintain eye contact while someone talks to him is a good social skill that will help him mix more effectively with others in the future. You may find that he doesn't appear to listen to you unless he is facing you, so position yourself in a way that ensures you are able to look at each other.

His imagination is developing fast and you can use this to stimulate his use of language.

For instance, you can talk to his toy animals and pretend that they reply to you – tell your child what they say and ask him to speak to them, too. He'll very quickly join in this type of imaginative play; soon he will be able to tell you their names and all sorts of things that have happened to them. A toy telephone serves the same purpose at this age. He'll

Below: Use moments when you have your child's full attention to point out and name familiar objects – like the parts of the body.

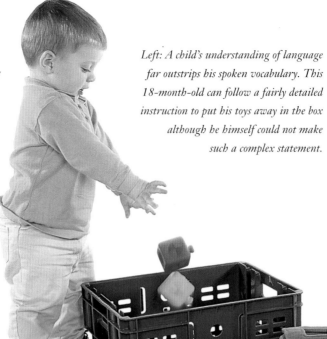

have great fun prattling away on the phone as he has an imaginary conversation with one of his friends or perhaps with a grandparent or another member of the family.

Although your toddler usually has quite a lot to say for himself, there may be times when he is frustratingly slow in communicating his ideas and feelings to you. Try not to rush him or he will just give up the idea altogether. Relax and let him take his time. He probably

Left: A child's understanding of language far outstrips his spoken vocabulary. This 18-month-old can follow a fairly detailed instruction to put his toys away in the box although he himself could not make such a complex statement.

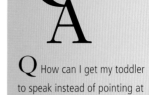

Q & A

Q How can I get my toddler to speak instead of pointing at what he wants?

A You can't force your child to speak but you can encourage his language development by not reacting to his non-verbal gestures. There is a greater incentive for him to speak when he finds that body language alone doesn't get the desired result. And when he does use words instead of pointing, always react quickly and praise his use of language.

Q My child talks to himself. Is this normal?

A Yes. One of the best ways for him to improve his language skills is through regular practice and what better way to practise free from interruption than by talking to himself? You won't understand most of what he says during these self-directed monologues, but remember that his words are not intended for you to hear.

Toys: dolls and cuddly toys, toy telephone, plastic cups and saucers, story books, bath toys

✦✦✦✦✦✦ Top·Tips ✦✦✦✦✦✦

1. Point out the names of the primary colours to him. While he is too young to learn the names of colours, your naming them can help him become aware of the differences between them.

2. Remove distractions when trying to attract his attention. There is absolutely no point in speaking to your toddler when he is totally engrossed in a television programme. Switch the set off for a moment while you talk to him.

3. Make a tape of familiar sounds. Tape record everyday sounds, such as a car driving past, a cup filling with water, and so on. Watch your child's face to see if he recognizes any of them – go through the tape again explaining each sound.

4. Miss out the last word of his favourite song. Sing all the song until you approach the very last word, and then stop. Look at your child with an expression of anticipation on your face – he'll try to say the missing word.

5. Look closely at your child when he speaks to you. Your toddler speaks because he has something important to say to you. Listen carefully and respond positively, even if much of what he said was unclear.

simply needs another few moments to find the words that he wants to use. Be as patient with him as you can.

At this age he starts to learn the names of the various parts of the body. A good time for teaching these words to him is at bathtime or when he undresses for bed. Make this activity informal and enjoyable, perhaps by stroking the palm of his hand when you tell him 'This is your hand' or gently touching his ear when you explain that 'This is your ear'. The same applies to names of familiar household objects. Instead of saying to your toddler 'Put these away', you could say 'Put these toys in the big box'. You will help to expand his range of vocabulary through your own use of language when you speak to him.

Stimulating Language: 19 to 21 Months

Progress in language continues and your child realizes that speech is not just for the purpose of communicating her ideas and feelings – it's also a good way to make social contact. She is increasingly interested in two-way conversation. Her broadening vocabulary and use of more complex sentence structures enable her to make more sophisticated contributions when you engage her in discussion.

Suitable Suggestions

Encourage your child to talk to you about events as they occur – don't wait until the end of the day to recap as she may have forgotten about the incident. Bear in mind that she is fascinated by everything going on around her, and has an inherent desire to speak to you about her experiences. Whether it is putting on her vest and pants in the morning or going out for a walk in the afternoon, your talkative toddler is delighted to chat to you about it and needs you to respond. Use clear language, with words that she can easily understand.

If you find your child is not particularly talkative at any point in the day, don't try to force her into having a conversation with

Above: Your child will initiate more conversations by commenting on what he is doing or something he sees.

you. Maybe she's tired or perhaps she is in a bad mood. Whatever the reason, let her have quiet times. You'll probably find that she becomes more communicative again later in the day.

You can also further your child's understanding of both receptive language (the language she understands when it is spoken to her) and expressive language (the

Left: Talking to your child during everyday activities will help increase his vocabulary and understanding.

Q My 21-month-old child has a stilted way of talking, as though abbreviating what she is saying. Is that typical for a child this age?

A Her language sounds abbreviated because it contains only the key words, such as 'want milk' or 'me sleep'. Over the next year she starts to add in other types of words such as prepositions and adjectives. This is the way in which language development normally progresses over the months.

Q My toddler speaks so hurriedly I can't make out what she says. What should I do?

A She is just impatient to express herself. Over the next few months she naturally slows down her speech and it will become easier to understand what she is saying. In the meantime, if she is over-excited when she speaks to you, try to encourage her to speak more slowly. But there is absolutely no cause for concern.

Toys: story books, tapes or CDs of children's songs, animals and farm buildings, toy cars, children's video tapes

Above: At this age your child may prefer to watch others than to talk to them.

Top·Tips

1. Ask her to name objects. Point to an object she knows and ask her what it is called. Gradually extend this to new objects that you haven't heard her name before – if she's not sure, tell her the word she is looking for.

2. Respond when she talks to you. Whether or not you fully understand what your 21-month-old toddler says to you, give her a positive response, such as a smile or a nod. She needs this sort of encouraging feedback from you.

3. Expect her to 'clam up' in company. Despite her instinctive desire for attention, your child may suddenly lose her confidence to speak when she is confronted by a sea of faces. She'll speak once she is alone with you again.

4. Use doll play. Give your toddler instructions for her doll. For instance, 'Put your doll over there' or 'Give your doll a drink'. This helps develop her ability to listen, to think, to interpret and then to act on what she has heard.

5. Sing songs together. Her increased speech and language skills mean that she can join in more easily when you sing songs to her. If you pick her favourites, you'll find that she tries to sing along too.

language she uses to voice her own ideas and feelings) by demonstrating the meanings of new words with which she is not fully familiar. For instance, if you want to say to her 'That man is very tall', raise your hands high at the same time so that she sees a visual interpretation of your comment. Words accompanied by a physical demonstration of their content enhances her grasp of their meaning.

Make up listening games to play with her. For instance, you can ask her to shut her eyes and to listen very carefully and tell you when she hears a car go past your house – if she doesn't get it right first time, let her try again. Or you could read her a story, substituting her name for the name of the central character, and ask her to let you know whenever she hears her name mentioned as you read. Any game at all that involves your child in focusing on listening closely for information will benefit her language development and provide lots of fun along the way.

Stimulating Language: 22 to 24 Months

Speech is very much part of his life now. By the time he reaches his second birthday your child is much more communicative, has a better grasp of vocabulary, grammar and sentence structure, and likes talking to other people. In particular, he enjoys mixing with other children of his own age, even though they can't always make themselves understood to each other.

HE STAMMERS

Stammering (also known as stuttering) is common in children as young as 2 years; a child of this age often starts to say a word, doesn't complete the whole word, starts to say it again, and so on. Repetitions and uncertainty like this occur frequently when a child's language development is beginning to accelerate. Fortunately, most 2-year-olds pass through their stammering phase without any help as their confidence grows.

If your young child stutters, make sure that nobody (including older siblings) makes fun of him, tries to mimic him, or attempts to hurry him along. He needs your time, patience and support to get through this temporary phase.

Suitable Suggestions

You continue to have a huge influence on your toddler's language development. You will find that he picks up the style of words and sentences you use. Try to make the language you use with your child basic but varied. Instead of using the same words each time, offer alternatives that have the same meaning. For instance, the word 'big' could sometimes be replaced by 'huge' or 'large', the word 'nice' could be replaced by 'good' or 'great' – your child takes his cue from you and when he hears you use different words

Below: Meals are a good time to introduce language concepts: naming different foods and their colours, whether things are tasty or nice, hot or cold and so on.

Right: At around 2 children begin to talk to each other more.

he'll start to do the same as well. This gradually broadens his vocabulary.

Expect your child to make plenty of mistakes with the language he uses – it's a normal part of the learning process. He will mix up words

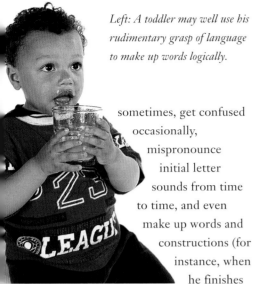

Left: A toddler may well use his rudimentary grasp of language to make up words logically.

sometimes, get confused occasionally, mispronounce initial letter sounds from time to time, and even make up words and constructions (for instance, when he finishes a glass of juice, he might say 'juice gonded', thereby creating an entirely new word for himself).

Don't correct him when he makes language mistakes or he may become anxious. A more effective strategy is to reiterate what he has tried to say, using the correct words or construction, as if you were agreeing with him rather than pointing out his mistake. If he watches a dog walk away from him and says, for instance, 'Doddy gone away' you could say 'Yes, that's right. The dog has gone away.' Modelling language in this way shows him how to say the words correctly, without weakening his self-confidence.

Your child expects everybody to understand him – he knows what he is trying to say and so he assumes you do as well. And he may explode with frustration when he suddenly thinks that you don't grasp his meaning. The more you ask him to repeat himself, the angrier he becomes. In this situation, use a variety of strategies. You might decide to distract his attention on to something else altogether, or you could just nod your head as though you have understand exactly what he has said.

✦✦✦✦✦✦ Top·Tips ✦✦✦✦✦✦

1. Let him speak at mealtimes. Whether eating on his own or with the rest of the family, encourage him to chat as he eats. The relaxed atmosphere, coupled with the pleasure of eating, is likely to make him particularly conversational.

2. Play tongue and lip exercises. Place him in front of a mirror and show him how to wiggle his tongue about, blow through his closed lips, and make 'p', 'b' and 'd' noises. This improves tongue and lip control.

3. Ask him to make up songs. Play a simple tune without words and suggest that he makes up his own words to accompany it. He may look at you in amazement at first, but once he gets the idea he will have great fun creating his own songs.

4. Show him recent family photographs. He studies photographs very closely when he recognizes people in them, and he loves to see pictures of himself. Use this as a stimulus to talk about the family events and holidays in the pictures, which he may partly remember.

5. Make occasional 'mistakes' when reading stories. To sharpen his listening skills, read a familiar story to him but change it in one small way (for instance, the name of the family pet) and wait for him to spot your error.

Below: Encourage your child to make up simple songs – it's a great way for him to play around with words.

Q&A

Q Why is it that my child says 'f' for 's' and also says 't' for 'c'?

A Say these sounds slowly yourself – you'll discover that 'f' and 't' involve your teeth, lips and the tip of your tongue, while 'c' and 's' involve the back of your mouth. Your child finds front-of-mouth sounds much easier at this age and hence makes these substitutions. He will gradually master the whole range of sounds.

Q Is it true that fairy stories can frighten a young child?

A Some stories have the potential to frighten your child. That's why it is important to choose carefully the books that you want to read to him, to ensure the content is appropriate for his age and understanding. He is unlikely to feel very positively about books and pictures if he experiences some that disturb him and make him afraid.

Toys: story books, picture cards of familiar objects, finger puppets, cuddly toys, craft and drawing materials

Stimulating Language: 25 to 30 Months

The sophistication of her language shows through in your child's everyday speech, as she starts to use pronouns (I, you, he/she, etc.) and descriptive words more consistently. She is able to hold conversations with other children of her own age, and she enjoys talking to adults as well. The minute details of family life fascinate her and she constantly asks questions.

Suitable Suggestions

Show interest in the endless tales that she brings to you, about this friend or about that toy. She is excited about everything that goes on around her and she wants to share this with you. You'll find that your child likes to sit beside you, cuddling up to you as she gives an account of her latest exploits. It's important that you respond with questions when she talks to you to let her know you are listening and are interested, and also to force her to think more deeply about the subject.

You can also use these conversations to help your child clarify her speech. For instance, when she starts to tell you about an incident involving another child at nursery or about an older sibling, she probably does so without actually mentioning the name of the child. Point out that she should name who she is talking about at the beginning. Of course she won't remember this immediately, but at least you are beginning to encourage her to plan her conversation and to think about the needs of the listener.

Now that her imagination is more advanced, try to involve her in pretend play, for example, dressing-up games. Your child thrives on this sort of activity and it provides

PLAYGROUP AND NURSERY

At this age, your child's language development can be enhanced by mixing with other children as much as it can by stimulation from you. Of course, she bickers sometimes with her peers when they play together, but for most of the time they prattle away happily to each other, sharing stories and experiences.

The incentive of communicating with a friend in order to play together is strong enough to prompt better speech and more mature listening skills. That's why it is so important for you to arrange regular contact with others her own age, at either a playgroup or nursery, or even during visits at home.

Above: Conversation with your child is now a two-way thing. She will enjoy telling you things but rely on your questions to draw her out further.

an opportunity for her to develop her language skills because she can pretend to be a completely different person. Observe her during this type of play – the chances are that when she dresses up as an adult, her voice tone changes and she uses different

Right: Stimulate her imagination by using dressing up clothes and by talking about characters that appear in stories and nursery rhymes.

words. She has great fun marching about the place using new forms of language as she pretends to be someone else.

When you don't let her do what she wants, she might try to shout you down – her instinctive reaction on hearing

✦✦✦✦✦✦✦ Top·Tips ✦✦✦✦✦✦✦

1. Make music together. Play along with her as she tries to get sounds out of her toy musical instruments. She likes blowing the trumpet and harmonica, and bashing the drum. Encourage her to sing as you make music together.

2. Talk to your child about the programmes she watches. When she has finished watching a television programme or a video, chat to her about the programme. Ask her basic questions such as the name of the central character.

3. Emphasize prepositions in your speech. You can help her understand the meaning of words like 'in', 'on' and 'under' by demonstrating them. For instance, show her how the food goes 'in' the cupboard, and how her plate goes 'on' the table.

4. Cuddle up together when reading a story. Physical contact is very soothing for both of you. Snuggling together during story time relaxes your child and settles her into a positive mood so that she is ready for listening and talking.

5. Play sorting games with your child. Take some familiar toys such as teddies, building blocks or books, and put them in a pile in front of her. Then ask her to give you all the teddies, for instance. She will demonstrate that she can group some objects.

something she doesn't like is to tell you to be quiet. Calm her, then continue to say what you wanted to say anyway. She eventually learns that you have as much right to speak as she has, even though she is unhappy with the message you convey to her. Once you've had your say, listen attentively to her response.

Below: Television programmes are much more valuable if you watch them with your child and then talk to him about them afterwards.

Q&A

Q What should we do about our child's lisp?

A Many children develop a temporary lisp while they acquire speech (in other words, they substitute 'th' for 's', 'f' for 'th' and so on). In most instances this speech pattern disappears spontaneously as they grow older. Therefore at this stage you should do nothing in particular, except provide appropriate speech patterns for her to copy.

Q Is it true that boys are somewhat slower in learning to speak than girls?

A Evidence from psychological studies confirms that, in general, girls acquire spoken language at an earlier age than boys and they also develop more complex language structures before boys. This is only a trend, though; it doesn't mean that every boy says his first word later than every girl. Much depends on the individual child.

Toys: plastic human figures, clothes for dressing up, toy zoo with animals, story books, music tapes or CDs, cuddly toys

Stimulating Language: 31 to 36 Months

By now your child has grasped all the basic language skills and the foundations are set for further advances in vocabulary and grammar – a process that will continue throughout the remainder of his childhood and into adulthood. He still has a lot to learn, but he is a fully fledged 'talker' at the age of 3.

NURSERY RHYMES

Many of the traditional nursery rhymes date back hundreds of years. For instance, 'Ring-a-Ring-o-Roses' refers to the Great Plague of London – the 'ring' is the red rash indicating the disease has started and the 'all fall down' line at the end is self-explanatory. And this is one childhood tradition that you really should endeavour to maintain.

Nursery rhymes promote your child's language through repetition, through developing his awareness of rhyme, through demonstrating the poetic quality of language and through showing him that language has a fun element. Some nursery rhymes are tongue-twisters (such as 'Peter Piper') and are great for improving his mastery of different sounds and varied pronunciations.

Suitable Suggestions

There are lots of ways you can help develop your child's ability to use language for the purpose of interpreting and explaining his experiences. For example, talk to him about the television programme he just watched; ask him questions about the story line, about the characters in it, and about his opinion of the programme. Questions like these make him use language in ways other than just telling you what he wants or doesn't want. You can do the same about his friends, by asking about them and why he likes them. You might be surprised at the thoughtfulness of explanations given by your 3-year-old.

You'll also find that his interest in words themselves intensifies. He starts to ask you questions about the meanings of different words, perhaps ones that he has heard you use or that he heard at nursery. The meaning of these words may be obvious to you, but not to him. So be patient, give him your attention, and answer appropriately. Particular words may fascinate your child for no apparent reason. One day he hears someone say something and the actual sound

Below: At around the age of 3 children begin to hold lengthier and more fluent conversations with each other as they interact more and more in play.

Right: There are lots of opportunities to introduce your child to the names of colours – especially when you are painting, drawing or using play doh.

combination of the word amuses him – before you know it he uses that word constantly, probably not accurately. Make sure he knows its real meaning.

Around this time, the focus of your child's language moves away from himself to include other people. It's no longer all about what he wants, or what happened to him, or what he thinks – his increasing social awareness turns his attention towards the feelings and reactions of others. This is a positive step forward, and you can enhance

this aspect of his language by providing lots of opportunities to mix with other children and adults. Apart from the obvious social experiences of playgroup or nursery, he benefits from mixing with siblings and with other family members of all ages. You might also consider enrolling him in a leisure activity class such as swimming or dancing, or whatever interests him. The speech and language he uses and hears in these varied contexts extend his own language skills even further.

✧✧✧✧✧✧✧ Top·Tips ✧✧✧✧✧✧✧

1. Start to teach individual colours.
Although he may not be able to name individual colours, he is probably able to sort them. Give him a pile of coloured bricks, hold up a red one, for example, and say to him 'Find another one like this'.

2. Give factual replies to his questions.
Investigations reveal that children in this age range mainly ask questions about facts rather than about feelings – it is a way of enhancing their knowledge. So give brief and accurate answers as required.

3. Choose stories that are more demanding. He is ready to listen to stories with more complex plots and multiple characters. Pick books that are interesting and at the level of your child's understanding – these will grab his interest.

4. Provide explanations. He is now at the age where he begins to understand explanations about why he should behave in a certain way. He is more likely to follow rules about behaviour when they are explained to him.

5. Talk about his drawings and modelling. When your child shows you his latest creative production – in paints, pencil or modelling material – chat to him about it. Listen appreciatively as he explains it to you in great detail.

Below: Talk to your child about what she is drawing – at this age she is likely to have a particular image in mind though you may not recognize it on paper.

Q & A

Q My 3-year-old still only uses single words, without forming short sentences. Is this normal at this age?

A The rate at which children acquire speech varies greatly. However, most children are further ahead with their language at this stage. The chances are your child's speech will develop normally and that there is nothing to worry about. But you may find it reassuring to have a chat with your family doctor about this.

Q At what age do children start understanding jokes?

A Humour develops from birth – your child probably first smiled at around six weeks. The use of language as a means of stimulating laughter starts around the age of 2. Although your 3-year-old's jokes may not strike you as funny – perhaps because they simply involve words in an unusual order – they make your child giggle.

🧸🚂 **Toys:** soft toys and dolls for imaginative play, sing-along tapes or CDs, story books, child-sized kitchen

Learning

The Development of Learning Skills

Your child's learning ability continues to grow rapidly during this phase of her life. A good way to define learning ability (also called 'learning skills', 'thinking skills' and 'cognition') is your child's ability to learn new skills and concepts, her ability to make sense of events that happen around her, her ability to use her memory accurately and her ability to solve small problems.

Every day you'll notice examples of how your child's reasoning skills, her understanding of new concepts and her problem-solving skills are developing throughout her second and third years. She becomes altogether better at both thinking and learning.

Here are some of the main changes to look for:

• **symbolism.** Until she reached 18 months or so, your growing child was unable to use symbols – in other words, she could only think in terms of here-and-now, and if an object was not physically in front of her she had difficulty thinking about it. But this changes mid-way through the second year, when she starts to think in images. The emergence of symbolism vastly increases the possibilities for learning.

• **attention.** Part of learning involves focusing on a piece of information long enough to extract meaning from it. Babies have a random attention

Right: Your child learns incidentally from her everyday experiences. So relax and have fun with her whenever you can.

span, but as your child nears the end of her second year she begins to exercise control over the attention she gives to an object or activity, and when something grabs her interest, she focuses on it until she has satisfied her curiosity.

• **memory.** The ability to recall previously learned information is an essential part of learning and this capacity increases in the second and third years. Both her short- and long-term memories become more effective. This allows her to remember recent experiences (something that happened perhaps a minute ago) and distant experiences (something that happened several months ago).

• **language.** Learning and language development are closely connected.

Your toddler's language explosion improves not only her communication skills but also her ability to learn. She uses language to ask questions, to test out her ideas, to reason, and to improve her understanding of the world.

Remember, however, that she continues to learn principally through explorative and discovery play and through listening, talking and discussing. It doesn't matter whether she plays with an empty box, with a bath toy, with her cutlery during meals, with a jigsaw, or in fact with anything at all – when she interacts playfully with

anything in her environment she learns new things. The same applies to language – she learns something new in every conversation she has. Look on her as a dynamic scientist, who soaks up information like a sponge and is then eager to put this new knowledge into practice.

Of course, there are specific things you can do to stimulate and promote your child's learning skills, but do keep in mind that a substantial amount of learning takes place every day just through your child following her normal routine. For example, getting dressed in the morning is a complex task involving sorting, matching, coordination, memory and concentration. Bit-by-bit, each day she learns more about dressing until she achieves a level of mastery at the age of 3 that seems light years ahead of her competence at the same task when she was only 15 months old.

Her View of the World

It's important not to make assumptions about your child's thought processes – despite her remarkable progress in learning as a young child, there are still two distinctive characteristics of her learning skills that are different from yours.

First, she doesn't fully understand cause and effect, and may identify a connection between two events where no such connection exists. This is partly due to her immature reasoning and partly due to her lack of experience. For instance, if a light goes out – perhaps because the bulb has broken – at the exact moment that she sneezes, your child may think that her sneeze has caused the lights to go off. Then in future you could find that every time she sneezes, she looks around anxiously waiting for something to happen to the lights!

When your child makes a comment about a cause-and-effect connection (for instance, when she tells you that she made the rain appear because it started when she put her coat on), you should explain clearly why the connection doesn't really exist. She might not believe you at first, so you will probably need to repeat your explanation later.

A second major difference in her thinking is that she still tends to see

Above: Prior to the age of 3 children are very self-absorbed and have little concept of how other people may feel.

things only from her own point of view. That's why your 2-year-old looks blankly at you when you reprimand her, for example, for playing with her older brother's toys when she was previously warned off. The rebuke 'How do you think your brother feels when you mess up his toys?' goes right over her head, because she isn't yet at the stage when she can easily see things from another person's perspective. She begins to be able to appreciate other points of view by the end of her third year.

Above: Much learning takes place through self-motivated exploratory play – often with everyday objects.

Learning

Age	Skill
15–18 Months	Your child is able to combine his hand–eye control, his concentration, his memory and his understanding in order to complete a complex task.
	He can recall without much difficulty where certain objects have been placed in the house, particularly if he uses them regularly or if they are his favourite items.
	His problem-solving skills enable him to meet challenges that were previously beyond him, and he practises the solutions again and again.
19–21 months	Wooden inset boards fascinate him and this type of toy is well within his capability, as a result of his developing reasoning and perceptual skills and his improved hand–eye control.
	He is no longer curious only about events happening in his immediate environment. Now his interest has extended to occurrences beyond the walls of his house.
	Cupboards and closed spaces trigger his curiosity. He has a boundless desire to know what is concealed behind those closed doors and will go to great lengths to find out.
22–24 months	He begins to understand that he can manipulate and arrange objects in order to achieve a desired result. However, his limited hand–eye coordination may sometimes inhibit him.
	Imaginative play shows through at this stage. He is able to create scenes and images in his head using toys as props to act them out.

From 15 Months to 3 Years

What to Do

Seat your child either in a high chair at a table or in his own child-sized chair and table. Build a tower with wooden bricks in front of him. Then give him some bricks and ask him to do the same. Depending on his mood, he might build a tower around three or four blocks high.

Ask your toddler to bring you his teddy from his bedroom. He can probably remember exactly where it is – even though he can't describe the location in words – and is able to toddle off immediately so he can comply with your request.

Find a small cardboard box with a lid, and put a couple of wooden bricks inside. After rattling the box in front of your toddler, let him explore it. You'll probably find he takes the lid off, empties the bricks out, then returns them to the box and puts the lid back on.

Give your toddler a solid wooden inset board – in which the wooden pieces fit inside a frame – and watch him try to assemble it. He'll probably succeed as long as there are no more than about five pieces. If he has difficulty at first, show him how to solve the puzzle.

If your toddler hears noises outside, perhaps in the garden or in the street, lift him up so that he can peer out of the window. You'll find he is completely engrossed by all that he sees.

Provide opportunities for your inquisitive toddler to explore whenever possible. Keep a special cupboard or box full of 'treasures' that he can safely investigate. However, he needs supervision. His lack of appreciation of danger means that if he finds a bottle of fluid, for example, his first reaction is to taste it. Have childproof locks on cupboards containing hazardous or breakable items.

Give your child a small plastic toy barrel that unscrews in the middle. Encourage him to watch you as you open the barrel, put a small toy inside, then screw it together. Hand the barrel to your child and ask him to get the toy out of it. He'll try hard.

Allow him to play with a doll's house with the little figures and furniture that go inside. He gives each tiny doll figure a name and moves furniture from room to room, as he gives this imaginative play his full concentration. Other toys such as toy vehicles and farms with miniature animals provide similar imaginative play opportunities.

Learning

Age	Skill

Your child watches you closely while you progress through the day and he occasionally copies your actions. He may do this for several minutes at a time.

25–30 months

He is beginning to understand the concept of money, although at this age this knowledge is still at a very elementary level. He hasn't yet grasped that each coin has an individual value.

Although he may not be able to explain to you in words why certain objects should be grouped together, he has developed the concept of classification.

Your child's broad sense of time begins to emerge. While an appreciation of hours and minutes is beyond him, he begins to understand larger units of time, such as days.

31–36 months

As his short- and long-term memories become more reliable he is able to recall and accurately discuss experiences that have occurred in the past.

Your child becomes more able to use his background knowledge and past experiences in order to anticipate the consequences of his actions, although he still acts impulsively.

He is able to make basic comparisons between two objects in terms of size or height. However, he still sometimes gets confused over this even by the time he reaches the age of 3.

From 15 Months to 3 Years

What to Do

Sit on a chair facing the mirror, and start to brush your hair. Ask your child to sit beside you. After staring at you for a couple of seconds, he'll begin to brush his own hair. Copying what you do is instinctive and makes him feel very important.

Show him a handful of coins, and ask him to tell you what they are. He may be able to tell you that they are 'money', but he won't be able to name any of the coins. Give him some realistic-looking plastic coins and notes to play shops with.

Place a small bundle of plastic animals and plastic bricks in front of your child. Say to him, 'Sort these out. Put one pile here and another pile here.' It is likely that he is able to sort them into a pile of bricks and a pile of animals, without the need for further explanation.

Tell him that you will take him to the park 'tomorrow'. The fact that he is excited at this promise and yet doesn't immediately rush to put his hat and coat on is confirmation that he knows the outing to the park is not now but in the future. You can encourage his appreciation of time by explaining future events in terms of familiar daily markers, saying 'after breakfast', for example.

Talk to your child about something that you both did yesterday – he'll remember. Then extend the conversation to something special that you did a couple of weeks ago (for instance, a visit to his grandparents). You'll probably find that his recall of that is also good.

Pose questions that encourage him to think ahead. For instance, 'What would happen if you filled the glass to the top and tried to lift it?' or 'Suppose you pushed that chair, what would happen next?' In most instances, he correctly anticipates the outcome of such events.

Take two glasses of equal size from the cupboard. Pour juice into one glass until it is almost full and pour only a small amount into the other glass. Tell your child to 'Show me the glass with the most juice in it.' He'll probably select the right one.

Stimulating Learning: 15 to 18 Months

Your child's increased learning skills enable her to take more control over her daily life. She begins to think for herself, tackling challenges with great enthusiasm. Her improved memory allows her to recall where she has previously placed items, for example. Concentration also improves and she plays with toys for longer, leaving her less dependent on constant stimulation from you.

LISTEN PLEASE

You probably find that your toddler occasionally fails to respond when you speak to her. The problem is that you compete against many other sources of stimulation. There's so much to attract your toddler's attention that it is hardly surprising that she doesn't always listen to you.

You can help develop her listening skills by putting a 'name' prompt into the sentence. For instance, if you want her to follow an instruction, start off by saying her name, and only deliver the instruction when she turns around and makes eye contact with you. The more she listens, the more she learns.

Suitable Suggestions

Your toddler likes to experiment with toys and she won't need much encouragement from you to do this, but be ready to offer suggestions anyway. Now is a good time for her to become more creative in the way she explores. She has the determination and self-confidence to be more varied in her responses; all she needs is a little guidance and prompting from you.

For instance, when she struggles to place a particularly awkward shape in the shape-sorter box, remind her that she can turn the shape around or that she could try alternative shapes for that hole. She may be unwilling at first to follow your advice because she'd rather achieve success without your help, but she'll give it a try eventually. The specific advice you offer her isn't so

important – what matters is that you have helped your toddler to think more creatively, approaching challenges from different perspectives.

Right: With some gentle guidance you can often help your child with something she finds tricky – turning potential frustration into achievement.

Left: By now your child will enjoy following a simple story and will respond to familiar characters.

Continue to develop her imaginative play even though her imagination is still limited. For instance, read her stories in a lively way, using different voices and varying the loudness depending on the action. You'll find that her facial expressions match yours as she listens to every word, synchronizing her mood with the mood you express. Do not make story-telling too dramatic, though, as toddlers may become so engrossed that they are upset by the emotions aroused.

Gradually improve your child's attention span, as this will help her general learning ability. One strategy is simply to sit by your toddler as she plays with her toys. There is evidence from psychological research that a child is likely to play for longer in the presence of a parent. Another strategy is to observe her at an activity, and when you see that she is ready to move on to something else, suggest that she continues with it for a little longer. Don't expect too much from her at this stage, though.

Below: Water play will enthral children of this age group and gives them a basic idea of volume and quantity.

✥✥✥✥✥✥✥ Top ∙ Tips ✥✥✥✥✥✥✥

1. Broaden her play interests. She'll learn best when she plays with a range of toys instead of focusing on just one or two. If you notice that she continually plays with the same few toys every day, try to engage her interest in other items.

2. Provide opportunities for water play. Whether at the time she has a bath or at some other point in the day, let your toddler play with cups and water. She'll learn about quantities and volume through the experience of filling and emptying containers of different sizes.

3. Look for gradual changes. Naturally you hope that she will progress rapidly with learning. Try to avoid placing too much pressure on her to learn new skills all the time or she may become anxious, intimidated and unable to learn. From time to time allow her to relax by undertaking an activity that she's already thoroughly mastered.

4. Practise new learning in short bursts. She learns best for short periods of time. For instance, several five-minute episodes of learning separated by 15-minute breaks is a better way to learn than one continuous session lasting an hour.

5. Give her time. Your stomach may churn with frustration as you watch your toddler try every solution to the puzzle except the right one. But don't rush in too early; she needs time to test out different strategies for herself.

Q What type of jigsaw should my 18-month-old toddler be able to manage?

A Although her learning and coordination skills have improved, she still finds jigsaws and similar puzzles very challenging. The typical child of this age successfully tackles inset boards with around four or five wooden pieces. However, she'll probably need practice before she is able to place all the pieces in the right place.

Q My toddler is impatient with learning. If she can't solve the puzzle, she has a tantrum. What should I do?

A Her desire to learn is so strong that she can't wait, and hence her rage when the solution isn't immediately available. Calm her first and then sit with her and teach her how to solve the problem. Finally, ask her to complete the activity under your supervision.

Toys: inset boards, story books, plastic shapes, construction bricks, sand and water tray, nesting cubes

Stimulating Learning: 19 to 21 Months

The principal change in your child's learning at this stage is that he becomes more outward-looking. Of course he has always been curious to learn, but now he looks further afield for stimulation. His confidence has grown, leaving him emotionally ready to tackle new learning challenges. He becomes more focused and determined – you'll discover that he becomes ever more motivated to finish what he starts.

OBJECT PERMANENCE

You know that when you put, say, a pullover into a drawer and then close the drawer, the pullover is still there even though you can't see it – that's what psychologists call 'object permanence'. It's not until your toddler is older than 18 months that he fully grasps this concept.

Before this stage, he would stop looking for an object that was out of his line of vision. It was a case of out of sight, out of mind. Now, however, he fully understands object permanence – so he looks for an object even though he didn't actually see where it was placed.

Suitable Suggestions

Feed his unquenchable thirst for new facts and new information. For several months he has been keen to explore all the hidden spaces of your house. Now is the time to broaden his sphere of interest. When you take your child shopping or to a friend's house – or anywhere at all – encourage him to look around, to pay attention to whatever is going on around him. The activity of a busy urban street, the hustle-and-bustle of life in the aisles of a typical supermarket, all contain new stimuli to enhance his learning. Talk to him about his surroundings, point out the different people and objects as you move along, and respond to his questions.

He loves play that involves getting his hands messy, such as painting, modelling, and sand and water play. Perhaps it's the tactile sensations he derives from immersing his hands in these substances that make these activities so pleasurable, or maybe it's just the chance to mess around without worrying about tidiness. Either way, he learns about

Below: Your child becomes more curious about the world around him and loves to watch others playing.

Above: Your child will love the texture of sand: running it through his fingers, raking, digging and moulding it.

♦♦♦♦♦♦♦ Top·Tips ♦♦♦♦♦♦♦

1. Engage him in conversation whenever possible. Talking with you stimulates his mind, helps him consider things that he might otherwise ignore and allows you to direct his thoughts on to specific topics. This is a good boost for his learning.

2. Reduce distractions. You can strengthen your child's ability to concentrate by reducing distractions while he plays. For instance, turn off the television while he plays with his toys, and perhaps remove some of the toys he isn't playing with.

3. Encourage him to explore. If your child is timid at times and is reluctant to investigate and explore on his own, say to him, for instance, 'Let's look and see what this is.' Your support gives him the confidence to be more adventurous.

4. Provide emotional support. His trial-and-error method of learning is effective, but results in some experiences of failure and frustration. Always be ready with a comforting cuddle when he doesn't achieve success in the way he had hoped.

5. Give him items to stimulate his use of symbolism. Toy vehicles, toy people or toy animals encourage him to play imaginatively, as he acts out scenes he makes up himself. Suggest he tries this, if he hasn't already thought of it himself.

shape, size and patterns while engaged in that form of play. Try to build this type of activity into his regular schedule.

Give him specific tasks to strengthen his memory. For instance, you could ask him 'Can you find your ball?' or you could say 'Bring me the cup from the kitchen.' He won't always carry out these instructions – in fact, you may find he doesn't return for ages, having completely forgotten what it was you asked him! Yet basic requests like these improve his short- and long-term memories.

At this age he needs to explore both to learn and to satisfy his curiosity. Yet you need to ensure he remains safe. So be prepared to declare boundaries or even no-go areas if you think your exploring toddler may be at risk of injury.

Below: Getting upset when things don't work out is very common at this age and your reassurance is extremely important.

Q Do children of this age understand about colours?

A Colour awareness is present at birth, and develops from that moment on. At this age, though, your child won't be able to name colours or even to sort different colours into groups. Yet he appreciates the different visual characteristics of different colours. Help this process along by naming the colour of his clothes as you dress him.

Q Is there an optimum amount of time my child should spend watching television daily?

A There's no 'ideal' amount of television because much depends on the type of programme he watches. Whatever the amount of time your growing child spends watching television, make sure the programmes are suitable for that age group, that he doesn't just watch the same programme over and over again, and that television doesn't crowd out other activities. You can use television programmes to enhance language and understanding by talking to him about what he has watched.

Toys: modelling clay or play doh, soft toys, shape puzzles, inset boards, toy figures, picture books, boxes with lids

Stimulating Learning: 22 to 24 Months

As she approaches the end of her second year, your child is more independent in all areas, including her thinking skills. She understands that she has some control over what happens around her and this increases her willingness to explore. Through imaginative play, she tests out new ideas, and you'll find that this is a favourite form of activity.

INTELLIGENCE TESTS

An intelligence test is a series of small tasks that some psychologists use to assess a child's learning skills. This form of assessment looks at learning abilities including memory, pattern recognition, reasoning, language and understanding. Intelligence tests are standardized, which means that an individual child's score is compared against the typical score for a child of her age.

Although these tests were once extremely popular, many psychologists don't use them nowadays because there are serious questions concerning the reliability and validity of such assessments. In addition, they are thought by some professionals to be too narrow, resulting in an inaccurate picture of the child's true learning potential.

Suitable Suggestions

Let her follow you around the house as you tidy up, make meals, watch television, make a phone call, or do any other routine activity. Your child learns by watching you closely, by asking you questions and by imitating your actions. So you should be prepared to have your 'shadow' trail you wherever you go and to explain things to her as you go along. For instance, tell her the reasons why you need to wash the vegetables you are preparing for the family's meal. Your child listens to these explanations attentively.

Encourage her to play with a range of puzzles. Try to find ones that are challenging but not so difficult that she gives up without trying. She is already familiar with inset

Below: Approaching 2, he will have a better idea of how to put things together. But don't be afraid to help if something is too complex for him to tackle alone.

boards and therefore feels confident enough to attempt unfamiliar ones with a greater number of pieces. You could give your child her first jigsaw – this should consist of only two pieces, which easily fit together and which are a good size for small hands to manipulate. She thrives on your praise when she shows you her completed solution.

You can improve her memory by asking her to find a familiar object. She enjoys helping you and likes the challenge. Make this into a game. For example, let her see you place the newspaper on the kitchen table. A few minutes later, when you are both in another room, pretend that you can't remember

Above: Start to teach him how things fit into groups like animals, birds, flowers, food and so on.

where you left it and ask her 'Where is the newspaper?' She thinks for a moment, hurriedly makes her way into the kitchen and returns proudly a few moments later.

Remind her to think about a puzzle and its possible solutions before trying to solve it. Of course she still needs to use trial-and-error techniques as part of her learning, but she has a greater ability to think before she acts. Encourage her to look at the puzzle before handling it and once she has spent a few seconds thinking about it, tell her to test her idea. If it doesn't work, she should think again and then try again.

Below: Your child is learning the rudiments of planning: if you ask him what he is going to do next when playing with blocks he may well tell you that he is going to make a tower, for example.

✦✦✦✦✦✦ Top·Tips ✦✦✦✦✦✦

1. Let her sit at a table. Your child is more likely to spend longer playing with her toys when she is seated comfortably at a table with her toys laid out in front of her but within easy reach.

2. Ask her to explain her actions before she carries them out. This encourages her to think ahead. For example, when you see she is about to build something with her construction bricks, ask her to tell you what she plans to make.

3. Chat about yesterday's routine. She enjoys your attention and will be happy to chat away to you about the previous day's activities. Pretend that you can't remember some of the things you did together, in order to prompt her recollection.

4. Start to talk about categories. You can help your child develop the ability to group items by emphasizing common groupings in your everyday conversation – she begins to understand there are categories of things called, for example, 'toys', 'clothes' and 'drinks'.

5. Have a settled time each day. Make a specific point of having a quiet time every day when you and your child sit in the same room, each engaged on your own leisure activity without any other distraction. This boosts her concentration span.

Q&A

Q Why is it that my 2-year-old remembers some things from months ago but not others?

A Memories are easier to retrieve when they are vivid, meaningful and exciting. That's why your child remembers her friend's party that she went to several months ago and yet can't recall what she watched on television yesterday. The more stimulating the experience, the more likely it is that her memory of it will endure.

Q Is it true that humour and intelligence are connected?

A Every child is capable of humour and laughter, irrespective of her learning skills. The fact that one child laughs more than another is due to personality differences, not intellectual differences. However, some verbal jokes involve a sophisticated understanding of language and therefore a child has to have achieved that level of development in order to appreciate the humour.

Toys: inset boards, jigsaws, shape boxes, floor puzzles, crayons and paper, set of toy tools or gardening implements

Stimulating Learning:
25 to 30 Months

What a transformation in your child's understanding of the world around him! As well as spending time with you, he loves the company of others his own age. Through playing together and talking with his peers, your child learns a whole range of skills more rapidly than he could do on his own. You may be surprised at the new ideas he acquires from other children.

Suitable Suggestions
Your child is as interested in the details as he is in the broad picture, which is why he seems so curious about every little thing. Foster this inquisitiveness by providing new sources of stimulation, such as visits to the zoo – or even just to a pet shop. Be ready to answer all his questions about why birds have feathers and he doesn't have any, why a tiger has stripes, and so on. And be ready to

Below: In pretend play a child will often act out what she has seen in real life.

break the news to him that he can't have a giraffe at home!

If you do buy him a small domestic pet such as a goldfish, he will sit quietly watching it swim round and round the bowl. The actions of the fish totally mesmerize him. This is a sign of his desire to learn. Suggest to him

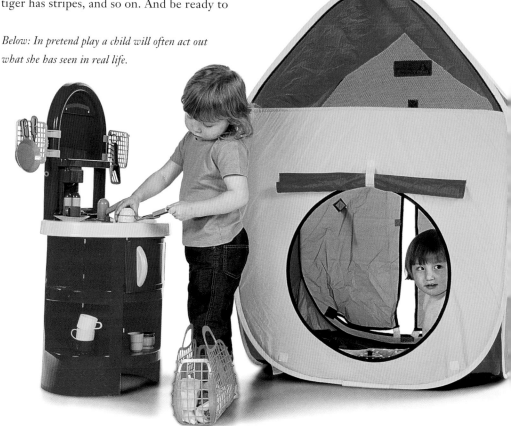

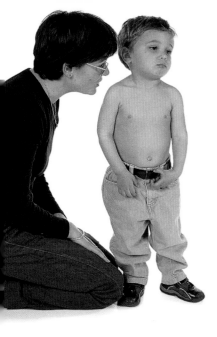

Above: Be understanding with difficult behaviour. It may be hard for him to understand the reasons for some rules.

that he draws a picture of the fish. Explain why the fish needs to be fed regularly and to have the water changed each week. Every detail matters to him.

You'll find his fascination with detail given full expression when he looks at picture books. He spots aspects of the picture that would previously have gone unnoticed simply because he wasn't mature enough to appreciate these elements. Now he misses nothing. Spend more time on each page, allowing him the opportunity to study each page in detail. Only go on to the next page when you feel he has extracted all the information he wants.

He loves pretend-playing situations that mimic real life, such as being in the kitchen or in a shop, and this boosts his learning. If possible, set up a play kitchen with as many toy implements as possible. Ask him to make a cake – he'll be only too pleased to mix up flour and water, to play with the mixture in his hands, and to pour it on to a plate for you to 'eat'. Similarly, he will enjoy playing in his own 'shop'. He will play with his friend, and act out buying things and getting change with toy coins and paper money.

Above: A safe outdoor environment where you can watch your child whilst allowing him the freedom to explore independently is great for his self-confidence.

Top·Tips

1. Don't restrict him too much. Allow your child to explore freely while under your supervision. However, safety must always remain your first priority. If he does aim for potentially dangerous territory, gently redirect him on to safer ground.

2. Name an object and ask your child to remember it. When he is settled at an activity, tell him something to remember, perhaps a type of food or a piece of clothing. After several minutes, ask him to recall the item you mentioned.

3. Read lots of stories to him. You'll find that he not only listens attentively but he now asks you a lot more questions about the events in the story as you read to him. Every so often, ask him what he thinks will happen next.

4. Show him recent family photographs. Ask him to identify the people in the snapshots, and then ask if he knows where the picture was taken. If necessary, give him prompts to jog his memory. He thoroughly enjoys this activity.

5. Practise colour matching. When you dress your child in the morning, set out three garments of different colours. Hold up a red item and say to your child 'Bring a pullover the same colour as this.' He may get it right!

Q & A

Q Is it true that the youngest child in a family usually possesses more creative thought processes than the oldest?

A There is evidence that second-born children and youngest children are often more creative thinkers than their first-born sibling. Whatever the explanation for this, you may find that your youngest thinks more flexibly and develops more innovative solutions to problems than his older brother or sister.

Q Does the fact that my child needs regular reminders about behaviour mean that he doesn't understand the rules or that he chooses to ignore them?

A He certainly knows the meaning of 'no' and probably understands more rules than you think. But his ability to use the information he has learned is affected by many factors, including his level of excitement and attention span. He easily forgets what he has learned if he becomes overwhelmed by other distractions.

Toys: toy household utensils and appliances, art and craft materials, large-piece jigsaw puzzles, construction kits

Stimulating Learning: 31 to 36 Months

Your child's learning skills become more advanced in the six months preceding her third birthday. Her memory has improved, she has an increasing ability to interpret the meaning of her experiences, and she has a vivid imagination, sound use of language and higher level of concentration. By the time she is 3, your child is ready to learn a whole range of new concepts.

SELF-FULFILLING PROPHECY

You have probably formed your own opinion of your child's abilities by now, and you may have already unconsciously decided whether she's bright, average, or even a slow learner. But this can create what psychologist's call 'a self-fulfilling prophecy'.

For instance, suppose, you think your child is not very clever. You'll expect less of her, and you'll accept lower achievements from her; this will probably de-motivate her, and sure enough your child's progress slows down. Your prediction becomes self-fulfilling. That's why it's vital to expect the most of your child's learning potential, and to continually provide a high level of stimulation for her.

Suitable Suggestions

Bear in mind that your child continues to learn from her everyday experiences with you and with other children, from her daily routine, and from her play activities. These remain key sources of natural stimulation. And now that she is more mature, she can happily sit quietly and focus her attention for longer periods, which increases her capacity to learn.

If your child is particularly restless during situations requiring concentration, help improve her attention span by sitting with her. Whenever you see her attention beginning to turn away, gentle reminders will help her focus on the activity in hand.

Play games specifically to extend and improve her memory. For instance, place approximately six household objects on a tray in front of your child. Ask her to look at the tray and try to remember all the objects.

Explain that you'll take the tray away, so she has to remember all the items she can. Remove the tray. You'll find that she probably recalls at least two or three objects, and quite possibly more. Once she has made her guess, let her look at the tray again.

Left: Your child's lively imagination will become increasingly obvious in her play.

You can improve your child's performance of this activity by teaching her the strategy of rehearsal. When she tries to memorize the objects on the tray, suggest to her that she says the names of the objects out loud, over and over again. This technique – which you probably use yourself when memorizing, say, a new telephone number – will increase her recall of the objects. She'll be pleased with the results. Likewise, when you give her a simple instruction to carry out, ask her to repeat the instruction back to you. This increases the

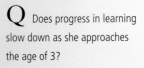

Above: At 36 months this little girl constantly absorbs ideas and information from her older sister.

✦✦✦✦✦✦✦ Top·Tips ✦✦✦✦✦✦✦

1. Teach early number concepts. Hand your child one toy brick and say 'That's one for you', then hand another and say 'That's two for you'. Your child may understand numbers up to three or four, even at this young age.

2. Give her sorting activities. For instance, ask your child to put her toy animals in one place and her toy people in another. You'll find that she can achieve this as long as she thinks carefully.

3. Continue to take an interest in her learning. She may be older and more mature but she still needs you to be proud of her attainments, and to praise her when she learns something new. Your child wants your approval.

4. Help her form classifications. For instance, say 'Tell me what you like to eat' and when she has named a few items, ask her to tell you more. If she includes a non-food product, say 'No, you don't eat that'.

5. Teach her to recognize her name in writing. Initially, she won't be able to tell the difference between her name and other written words. Point it out to her, and encourage her to find the same word elsewhere on the piece of paper.

amount of information stored in her short-term memory.

As well as reading stories to your child, suggest that she makes up a story to tell you. This encourages her to use symbolic thought, to draw on previous experiences and long-term memories, to blend concepts, and to try out new language structures. Her make-believe story may be hard to follow but it is an active use of her existing learning skills.

Above: At this age your child will still particularly enjoy sharing activities and books with his parents.

 Q & A

Q Does progress in learning slow down as she approaches the age of 3?

A No. Your child's rate of learning actually increases because she can think about concepts that were meaningless to her before. For instance, she starts to grasp the meaning of numbers and the significance of size and time. She may also recognize that letters and words have shapes, which is an early stage of learning to read.

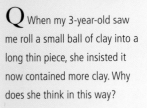

Q When my 3-year-old saw me roll a small ball of clay into a long thin piece, she insisted it now contained more clay. Why does she think in this way?

A Your child doesn't understand that the amount of clay remains the same no matter what its shape. She does notice that the thin shape is longer, however, and she mistakenly concludes that it must therefore have more clay in it.

Toys: toy figures and vehicles, colour- and shape-matching games, eight-piece form boards, larger jigsaws, dressing-up clothes

Social and

Emotional
Development

The Importance of Social and Emotional Development

By the age of 15 months your child's personality characteristics are showing through clearly and you are able to anticipate how he will react when he, say, meets strangers or can't find a toy he looks for, or when things don't go according to plan. His social and emotional development enters a new phase at this time as his own identity begins to develop. He wants to make choices, to do things by himself, and he can be very assertive.

As you will quickly discover, your toddler likes to get his own way. From the age of about 15 months onwards, he becomes very self-absorbed. When he wants something, he expects to get it right away and he isn't bothered by the fact that you are worn out or that he's been nagging at you all day. As far as your growing child is concerned, he comes first and your thoughts and feelings don't exist.

And it's not just that he would prefer to be in charge – he insists on it. If you don't let him do what he wants he may explode with

Left: Toddlers are by nature egocentric and are therefore often self-focused.

temper. It's almost as if your child is outraged by your impertinence at not doing what he wants you to do at the exact moment he wants you to do it. The dogged determination of your furious toddler knows absolutely no limits.

Toddler Egocentricity

Although this type of behaviour in an adult would be described as selfishness, that description doesn't apply when it comes to a child of this age. His behaviour is 'egocentric' in the true sense of the word, rather than 'selfish'. He is egocentric because he literally cannot understand anybody else's point of view. There have been many psychological investigations that confirm that children of this age struggle to consider how other people think and feel.

This stage of egocentricity – which may last until around the age of 3 or 4 years – affects your child's social and emotional development in a number of ways:

• **low tolerance of frustration.** His egocentricity means that he is totally shocked the moment his wishes are blocked, whether by you or because he simply can't achieve his target. He may experience a sudden surge of frustration that overwhelms him – he just can't believe that he can't get what he wants, when he wants it.

• **social indifference.** When you observe your 15-month-old toddler playing in the company of other children of the same age, you'll

Above: Before the age of 3 your child may spend much of his time focused on his own activities rather than playing with others.

notice how unaware they are of each other's feelings. Egocentricity means that one child will thoughtlessly snatch a toy from another child's hand without asking simply because he wants to have it.

• **frequent anger.** When you have to draw the line with your child aged 2 or 3 years, he'll probably be furious with you. He can't accept that you have set rules for him to follow; from his perspective, his feelings come first and it doesn't matter to him that you are the parent and he is the child.

Remember, though, that your toddler is still a wonderful, loving child who gives much love to you and to others in his family. Despite an increase in tantrums and other frustrations, there are plenty of times when he is settled and when you have great fun just enjoying his company. Enjoy these frequent moments, and do your best to avoid them becoming overshadowed by the more challenging episodes.

Vulnerability

Despite this surge of determination and independence, your toddler remains vulnerable socially and emotionally. This same child, who only a few minutes ago howled at you angrily because you had the nerve to ask him to stop playing with his toys in order to prepare for his bath, now clings to you sobbing because he can't find his favourite cuddly toy. Self-confidence is easily rocked at this stage, turning happiness into distress, laughter into tears, in the flicker of an eye.

And the same applies to your child's sociability. You will have noticed that he enjoys the company of other children, although he doesn't yet have the social skills necessary to play cooperatively with them. When he is with his peers, he stares at them curiously and appears comfortable and contented in their company. But all it takes is another toddler to approach him unexpectedly, and before you know it he rushes over to you for protection because he is afraid.

Support and Sensitivity

This contrast between the assertiveness and determination of your growing child and his obvious emotional vulnerability means that you need to handle his changing moods sensitively. On the one hand, his temper tantrums will push you to the absolute limits of your tolerance and you will need plenty of resolve to withstand his demands. On the other hand, he needs your

Above: A 3-year-old can seem incredibly self-confident, but this is easily dented if he comes across something he is unsure about.

affection and support when he is upset.

You can help your child by teaching him what is acceptable behaviour and what is not, by giving him lots of love to increase his sense of security, by offering him help and advice when he faces challenges that are too demanding, and by suggesting ways that he can learn to mix better with other children.

Below: Remember that however trying your toddler can be at times, your love and attention is central to her happiness and her progress.

Social and Emotional Development

Age	Skill
15–18 months	She starts to assert herself and demonstrates her determination by trying to stamp her authority over you. Tantrums are common at this age.
	She wants to do more for herself in the key areas of her life, especially with feeding and dressing.
	Your child is fascinated by other children, watching them closely when in their company.
19–21 months	She shows signs that she is nearly ready to begin toilet training, although her bladder control is unlikely to be mature enough actually to begin the process.
	Your toddler's increasing assertiveness makes her challenge you, and her frustration with your refusal to do what she wants may show through.
	Your child makes more of an effort to engage you either by talking to you or by involving you in her play activities. She appreciates your company more now.
22–24 months	Two-year-olds are not very good at sharing. Your child might think it's fine to take a toy from another child without asking, yet she cries when the child does the same thing to her.
	She generally does more for herself around the house. Her skill at feeding herself is increasing and she has started toilet training now, although she may not yet be fully dry during the day.

From 15 Months to 3 Years

What to Do

Help her manage her assertiveness and inevitable frustrations more effectively by responding patiently and calmly to her demands. When she is furious with you because you have said 'no', stick to the limits you have set. She needs you to be consistent.

Encourage your child to hold the spoon in her hand so that she can try to feed herself. This is challenging for her but she'll manage to get most of the food into her mouth without spilling too much on to the table. Feeding herself is an important step towards achieving greater independence.

Provide social play opportunities for her, either at a parent-and-toddler group or at a friend's house. Don't expect her to interact with her peers, however, because she doesn't know how to be sociable yet.

Look for signs of readiness for potty training, such as your child telling you that her nappy is wet, or if she asks you to change her nappy because she feels uncomfortable in it, or if you find that the nappy is still dry after several hours. Buy a potty so that your child is familiar with it by the time she is ready to start using it.

Your toddler may put up a valiant effort to make you change your mind about something. If she does have a tantrum, resist the temptation to give in, or she'll have an even bigger tantrum the next time around.

Respond positively when your toddler tries to make conversation with you. Even though you might not fully understand what she says, make good eye contact and look interested in her comments. Make a particular point of playing with her every day.

Be patient with her when she becomes upset playing with other children. Encourage her to share toys, reassure her that she'll get the toy back in a few minutes, comfort her if she is upset about sharing and then return her to the play situation. The more contact she has with other children, the quicker she'll learn sharing skills.

Promote your child's increasing independence in her daily care. At mealtimes, encourage her to use a spoon to feed herself and to drink from an open cup that is at least half full. And let her help 'wash' herself at bathtime. This results in a surge in her self-confidence and willingness to try new activities.

Social and Emotional Development

Age	Skill
	Temporary separations from you may be difficult for her, and she might cry and cling to you the moment she realizes you intend to leave her with someone else.
25–30 months	Self-help skills have improved even further. She enjoys the new-found freedom that independence brings, though she continues to rely on you a great deal of the time.
	Having progressed through the stage of solitary play (where she plays on her own), she now plays alongside others and even attempts to play with them at times.
	Her willingness to explore on her own and to try more things on her own also results in more experience of frustration and failure. She may be despondent at times.
31–36 months	Your child is likely to be reliably clean and dry during the day (though there will be occasional 'accidents'), and you may want to consider starting night training as well.
	Despite her lack of mature social skills, your child may start to form a special friendship with one child in particular, probably the one she sees most regularly.
	She is becoming more aware of other people's feelings, especially when they are unhappy, and she makes a positive effort to help and comfort someone in distress.

From 15 Months to 3 Years

What to Do

Be prepared to leave your child briefly in the care of a reliable person, such as a trustworthy babysitter, relative or friend. If your child does appear upset at the moment of separation from you, reassure her, give her a big cuddle and then leave. Remember, she'll soon stop crying once you've gone.

Actively involve your child in dressing and undressing. For instance, teach her how to pull down her trousers and pants to go to the toilet, and how to pull off her socks and pullover when getting ready for bed. Expect her to be tidier in her eating habits.

Be ready to support your child when she plays with her peers. Disagreements can quickly develop simply because children of this age don't understand the normal social rules. Sort out arguments as quickly as possible, then encourage her to continue playing.

Choose activities and toys of an appropriate level for her capabilities. When a challenge proves beyond her, point out to your child that she need not get upset. Suggest that she tries again, using another strategy to solve the problem she faces. Keep her calm, and give her lots of praise when she does try a second time.

Remember that control of bowel and bladder at night is achieved after daytime control. If you find that your child's nappy is dry in the morning when she wakes up, suggest to her that she could try leaving the nappy off at nights. Never get upset with your child over the inevitable wet beds.

If your child does show a preference for one child, do your best to encourage that friendship by providing lots of chances for them to play together. However, make sure that she also plays with other children, too, as friendships change very easily at this age.

Watch her behaviour towards another child in tears. She approaches him with a sad, concerned expression on her face and asks what is making him cry. Your child may offer him her own cuddly toy because that makes her feel better when she's upset.

Stimulating Social and Emotional Development: 15 to 18 Months

Your toddler becomes more assertive during this period. He wants to do more on his own and he may become annoyed when you set limits on his behaviour. Tantrums may be frequent when he can't get his own way. He is getting more interested in other children, and will play alongside others his own age, although he won't actually interact with them.

COMFORTERS

Some children form an attachment to a cuddly toy or an item such as a blanket, or continue to suck a dummy long after they have stopped bottle- or breast-feeding, or develop the habit of sucking their thumb or twiddling their hair. This is a normal pattern of behaviour, and is nothing to worry about.

Psychologists believe that comforters of this sort give your child extra security at times when he particularly needs it, perhaps when he's tired, in unfamiliar surroundings or when going to bed. Most children grow out of this behaviour by the time they are 3 or 4.

Suitable Suggestions

The best strategy to enhance your toddler's social development is to provide opportunities for him to mix with others of his own age. The fact that he plays alone in social situations like this doesn't reduce the importance of this contact – he learns from watching other children's behaviour and from studying the different ways in which they play with toys.

Below: Though these toddlers are happy to play in proximity to each other they are all involved in their own separate activities.

One of the most popular ways to provide social contact is by taking him to a local parent-and-toddler group. As you are with him throughout his time in the group, your presence will give him enough confidence to attend without tears. Going regularly gets him used to being in larger groups of people, which in turn builds his social confidence. If there isn't a local group, invite parents of children the same age to your house so that all the toddlers can play together. And, of course, accept social invitations on your child's behalf. These social contacts are great for parents, too, providing opportunities to share experiences and talk through problems.

Right: At this age your child will begin to show preferences for particular toys and have a clearer idea of what he wants.

His identity builds more firmly now. This shows in a number of ways. For instance, he starts to pick the toys he wants to play with himself, instead of waiting to be guided by your choice; he takes more initiative in aspects of personal independence, such as feeding and dressing; and he probably asks for specific foods at mealtimes.

When your toddler expresses his own preferences, he isn't being deliberately awkward – it's just that he is beginning to think for himself. His drive for independence can be difficult for you, especially when he starts to make choices that clash with your own plans, but the development of his individual identity is an essential part of the growing process and is something to be encouraged. Naturally your child can't have everything he wants. Yet you can help him in his drive for self-reliance by giving him the chance to make small choices.

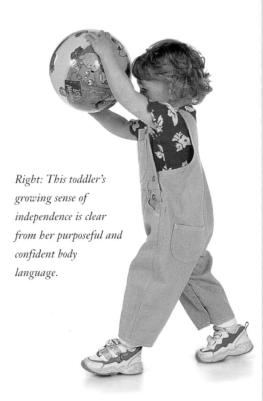

Right: This toddler's growing sense of independence is clear from her purposeful and confident body language.

✦✦✦✦✦✦ Top ✦ Tips ✦✦✦✦✦✦

1. Improve his social skills. Suggest that when he is with other children he should move towards them instead of staying beside you all the time. Tell him to pass a toy to another child when they are together in the same room.

2. Praise appropriate social behaviour. When your child acts positively in a social setting (for instance, if he shares a toy, or smiles at another child) give him a cuddle to show him that you are pleased with his behaviour.

3. Let him try new challenges. If he insists that he can do something by himself, stand back and let him make the attempt (as long as he is not in danger). He learns a lot about himself and his abilities through direct experience.

4. Deal calmly with jealousy. You may find that he becomes annoyed when he sees you talk to another child, because he likes to keep you all to himself. Calm his agitation, give him a big hug and reassure him that his special place in your affections is not threatened.

5. Include your toddler at family meals. Whenever possible, have your child sit at the family table for meals. Although he may be demanding, he will learn more quickly from example how to behave at the table than if he eats alone.

Q My toddler insists on having a night light. Should I discourage this?

A There's no harm in having a night light, although you can gradually reduce his reliance on it by fitting a dimmer switch. Make the light slightly dimmer each night, in such small stages that he doesn't realize you are doing this. You'll soon reach a point when he falls asleep without any light.

Q What can I do about my 16-month-old who refuses to leave my side at toddler group?

A Be patient with him, despite your embarrassment at his behaviour. He's obviously not ready yet to venture into the playroom alone. In the meantime, let him stay at your side. Almost certainly his natural curiosity will eventually take over and he'll soon start to drift slowly away from your side towards the exciting activities on offer elsewhere.

Toys: cuddly toys, toy musical instruments, inset boards, toy telephone with receiver, books with pictures

Stimulating Social and Emotion Development: 19 to 21 Months

Your child's developing sense of self makes her increasingly determined to challenge the rules and structures that you set for her at home. She is willing to push further than before, despite your insistence that she should follow what you say. Yet this apparent self-confidence can crumble very quickly indeed – all it takes is a small disappointment to send her rushing to you for a reassuring cuddle.

DISCIPLINE

It's a mistake to think that discipline is principally about punishment of misbehaviour. In fact, the word 'discipline' derives from the Latin word which means 'learning' – in other words, you should aim to create a system of rules at home that enables your child to learn how to behave appropriately.

Rote learning of rules, however, is not the most effective way of teaching your child good discipline. If your child knows a rule without having any understanding of why there is such a rule in the first place, then she'll probably break it the moment your back is turned. Always try to explain in simple terms the purpose of the rules you lay down for your child.

Suitable Suggestions

The irony about this phase is that the more your child tries to break the rules you set for her (for instance, by continuing when you ask her to stop, by demanding more sweets when you have told her that she's had enough, by touching that fragile ornament when you have said to leave it alone), the more she needs you to stick to the rules. A child raised in an environment where she determines the rules may become insecure and unhappy because of the lack of structure and consistency.

This means that you should be prepared to meet your toddler's assertiveness head-on, without losing your temper. Remind

Above: The playground is a good place for children to mix – ownership of toys is not such an issue and there are always exciting distractions.

yourself that it is in her long-term interests to follow rules of behaviour. After all, other children will not want to play with her later on if she thinks only of herself.

Left: If you can encourage your child to share toys at this early stage, it will make things easier for both of you in the long run.

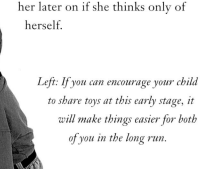

Above: You may find that your child begins to put more physical distance between you and him as he goes off to explore in the park or playgroup.

Be ready to offer advice in social situations because the solution that is obvious to you may not be obvious to her. It may not occur to her that, for example, she should say 'hello' to a child who approaches her. So give her plenty of basic social guidance.

The same applies to play. She might not realize that to let another child play with her toys is an effective social skill. The chances are that she isn't ready to follow all your advice, but starting to give her pointers about social interaction at least gets her thinking about these matters.

She expresses her ever-growing desire for independence in many ways. For example, she might hit your hand away when you try to help with feeding. Now is a good time to look for signs that she is ready for toilet training. Remember, though, that every child is different and that although many children start toilet training at around 21 months, there are some who are not really ready to start until later.

❖❖❖❖❖❖ Top ∙ Tips ❖❖❖❖❖❖

1. Believe in your parenting skills. Tell yourself that you are an effective parent, especially when your demanding toddler gets you down. Do your best to keep a high level of self-confidence so that you feel able to manage her competently.

2. Enjoy her company. She loves spending time with you. Listen to her as she tries to tell you her latest exciting piece of news, and play games with her. She needs to know that you care for her as much as ever.

3. Structure her day. Your child likes to have some predictability in her day. For instance, you might have meals within a set time range each day, or you may allow her to watch a video tape each morning. Routine makes her feel secure.

4. Comfort her when she is distressed. You may be surprised to hear her crying when you saw her playing contentedly only a minute before. She may quickly become upset by something that seems trivial to you but seems huge to her.

5. Keep explanations of rules basic. Your toddler at this age understands simple explanations such as 'Don't hit me because it hurts me and makes me cry'. Offer explanations that spell out the implications of her actions in terms she understands.

Q&A

Q Why does my 19-month-old toddler still wake up several times each night, calling for a drink?

A She probably wakes up so often because she enjoys your attention. When you go to her during the night, make sure that you don't lift her out of bed or give her a drink; instead calm her, without taking her from her bed. Her habit of night waking will gradually diminish if you use this strategy.

Q I feel as though I'm in constant confrontation with my toddler every day. What can I do?

A Try to take a more positive approach. Start to use more praise for good behaviour instead of reprimands for misbehaviour; make a point of spending time together just having fun; and do your best to keep any disagreements short so that anger between you and your toddler doesn't carry on for hours.

Toys: song tapes and CDs, modelling clay or play doh, toy versions of household tools, pull-along toys on wheels, shape-sorters

Stimulating Social and Emotional Development: 22 to 24 Months

Your child becomes much more sociable as he approaches his second birthday, although many of his contacts with other children still end up in tears – usually due to squabbles over toys. He may be shy with strangers and may greet relatives he hasn't seen for a while with a blank silence. He is more adept at feeding himself (although he still makes a mess) and he may well be reliably clean and dry during the day.

CRITICISM

Regularly criticizing your child for his misbehaviour reduces his self-confidence and creates a bad atmosphere for everyone at home. When you want him to change his behaviour, merge your negative observation with a more positive comment.

For instance, instead of saying 'You're naughty for leaving such a mess' you could say 'I'm surprised at this mess because you normally tidy your toys away'. Avoid criticizing your 2-year-old as a person ('You're horrible for doing that'), which may make him feel unloved. Instead focus on your disapproval of his behaviour ('I love you but I don't like what you did').

Suitable Suggestions

People talk of the 'terrible twos' when referring to this stage of development because it is associated with difficult and challenging behaviour. And there's no doubt that there is an element of truth in this observation. For example, dealing with your child's tantrum in the middle of a supermarket checkout queue (because he demands a bar of chocolate that is temptingly stacked where he can see it) is extremely embarrassing. He can appear completely unreasonable at times. Living with a tempestuous 2-year-old tests the patience of the calmest parent. But try to maintain a positive perspective no matter how despairing you may feel at times with his behaviour.

Right: Your 2-year-old is now likely to be developing a more sophisticated sense of humour, so you can share more jokes with him.

Reassure yourself that this behaviour – albeit infuriating – is normal and that it does not mean your are an inadequate parent or that you are doing anything wrong. Of course, cultivating this attitude won't have any direct effect on your 2-year-old's behaviour, but it may help you feel better about yourself. Make an effort to look for the more endearing qualities of your growing child, such as his sense of humour, his caring personality and his never-ending curiosity. This helps you maintain a balanced outlook on parenthood.

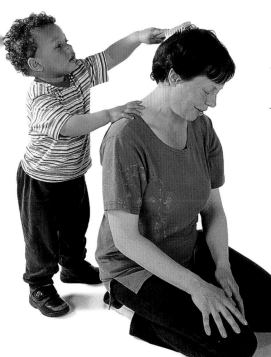

Left: Turn the tables sometimes and let your child brush your hair or help you get dressed by fetching your shoes – he will relish the responsibility.

By now your child probably has good bowel and bladder control during the day, and he is pleased that he now wears pants 'like a big boy'. He continues to need lots of praise and encouragement for his successes with the potty, however; give plenty of reassurance when he occasionally wets himself accidentally. His bowel and bladder control will improve as long as his self-confidence remains high.

Friendships start to play a more important role in his life now. He enjoys being with other children and you may find that he becomes bored, fractious and moody when he spends too much time on his own. On the other hand, don't be surprised to find that he and his friends bicker frequently, though do your best to sort out any squabbles. At this age, children don't bear grudges and quickly forget earlier disagreements. Try to make arrangements so that he has someone of his own age to play with most days.

Above: Never let potty training be something you get cross about. It will upset your child and success in this area depends very much on his level of confidence.

◇◇◇◇◇◇◇ Top ◇ Tips ◇◇◇◇◇◇◇

1. Let your child see that you value his achievements. His self-confidence depends greatly on how he thinks you view him – he needs to feel valued by you. He feels good about himself when you praise him and give him your attention.

2. Encourage him to think of others. He will become more sensitive to the feelings of other people if you specifically suggest this to him. Ask your child to think about the children he mixes with and to think of the games they could play.

3. Give him small tasks of responsibility. Even at this age, you can tell him that he's in charge of putting his toys into the toy box. Small amounts of responsibility like this increase his maturity and level of independence.

4. Teach him how to take turns. This very important social skill is one that you can practise with him at home. Give him experience of waiting to have a drink until you have had one, or letting his sister speak before him.

5. Make time for yourself each day. You need time just for you alone. You will feel more able to deal with your 2-year-old's fluctuating behaviour when you also have time for yourself, just to put your feet up.

Q Why does my toddler refuse to apologize when he does something wrong?

A You expect too much of your child by insisting on an apology. You can't force him to speak the words you want to hear. Instead, make sure that he knows you are unhappy with his actions and that you will be furious if he does the same thing again.

Q How can I make my child less timid when he is with other children?

A There are some techniques to consider. Do not allow him to avoid social interactions; reassure him that the other children will like him and will want to play with him; and arrange for him to play with only one child at a time instead of a group. These strategies may help to reduce his timidity.

🧸🚚 **Toys:** dressing-up clothes, books with pictures, large play-mat, construction toys, stacking toys, inset boards, picture cards

Stimulating Social and Emotional Development: 25 to 30 Months

Your child's social development advances as she becomes more able to get on with other children. She is keen to play with her friends and they interact together more effectively. You'll probably notice that she is more caring towards another child who is upset. However, alongside her increasing independence, during her third year you may also find that she becomes anxious about situations with which she previously dealt confidently.

FEARS

Evidence from studies suggests that most children develop at least one fear during the pre-school years, though girls tend to have more fears than boys. Fears develop at this age as a result of a combination of the child's very active imagination and her fluctuating confidence.

Typical fears of a child aged around 30 months include fear of small animals that move quickly, and fear of darkness. These fears tend to appear very quickly and also vanish very quickly. You can help your child get over a fear by supporting her, by encouraging her to face it, and by not making fun of her.

Suitable Suggestions

At this age your child may exhibit increased anxiety when temporarily separated from you, perhaps when you go out and leave her in the care of a babysitter or relative. It's surprising to see her become tearful at the prospect of parting from you for a short time – especially when you did not see this sort of behaviour from her when she was younger. This new anxiety may be because she is so

Left: If your child goes through a clingy period and doesn't want you to leave, give him as much comfort and reassurance as you can.

attached to you and now has the imagination to worry about coping without you.

If your child does seem likely to become tearful when she realizes you are off somewhere without her, then try to calm her at the moment of departure. Reprimanding or making fun of her for what appears to be immature behaviour only makes matters worse. Instead, give her a firm cuddle, tell her that you will be back soon and that you will hear about all the games she played while you were away, and then leave whether or not she cries. Lingering with your child until she settles completely might actually make the situation more stressful for her – a brief,

Right: Introduce 'sharing' by encouraging your child to offer food to others – if she also has a biscuit she'll be happy to do this.

Above: Sharing toys and equipment with other children is always likely to cause tension – but persevere with the idea of taking turns.

affectionate separation is more likely to build confidence in the long run.

She is better at sharing but still finds this social skill hard to put into practice. While she happily takes sweets and toys from her friend, the chances are that she clings tightly to her own possessions. She may not grasp that sharing should be reciprocal! Talk to her about this and encourage her to share under your supervision. For instance, watch as she shares some sweets with her brother and sister or friends. In general, petty bickering with her peers diminishes.

If she isn't already assisting with dressing and undressing, now is the time to get her interested in this activity. It really doesn't matter how much she does – whether she tries to put on her vest and pants by herself or barely pulls her socks off her feet – just as long as she shares the responsibility for this activity. Don't do everything for her simply because it's easier and quicker for you.

Below: Succeeding in an endeavour – like learning to use a slide – will encourage a child to take on other new challenges.

❖❖❖❖❖❖❖ Top·Tips ❖❖❖❖❖❖❖

1. Help her achieve success. There is nothing like success to make her feel confident. So guide her when she tries to complete a puzzle toy or when she does something to increase her independence – she loves the taste of success and it will spur her to continue with that activity.

2. Have loving physical contact with her. She's not too old to enjoy a loving, warm cuddle while you read a story to her. Close contact makes the activity much more enjoyable for both of you.

3. Comment on her strengths, not her weaknesses. Your child is likely to feel sorry for herself when she can't achieve her goal. When she is feeling negative, tell her the reasons why you think she's fabulous. You won't 'spoil' her with praise.

4. Listen when she talks to you. Once she has finished playing with other children her own age, she will want to tell you all about what happened. Listen attentively to her observations, nodding and frowning in all the right places.

5. Discourage rude behaviour. Your child might not know that it's rude to push to the front of a queue or to point at a spot on someone's face. She depends on you to teach her 'manners' at this age.

Q Is it true that girls are generally more caring towards others than boys at this age?

A Psychologists researching this question have indeed found this difference is present between boys and girls. The most likely explanation is that girls are encouraged to be caring and nurturing by their parents right from birth, and conversely, that aggressive behaviour is more tolerated from boys than from girls.

Q Is it normal for a child of this age to feel jealousy?

A Yes – jealousy is a normal human emotion. You'll see it in your child, for example, when you show interest in another child instead of her. When your child exhibits jealousy, reassure her and settle her. She learns to control her jealousy through experience.

🧸🚂 **Toys:** water and sand trays, modelling clay, crayons and paper, soft ball, toy car

Stimulating Social and Emotional Development: 31 to 36 Months

He is an altogether more caring, sociable and sensitive child as he reaches his third birthday. Friendships are regarded as important and he looks forward to seeing his friends each day, whether at home or at playgroup or nursery. Tantrums are less frequent and less intense, as he gains a better understanding that the world does not always revolve around him.

WHEN HE'S UNHAPPY

Every 3-year-old has moments of temporary unhappiness, but these negative feelings soon pass. If he appears continually unhappy, do you best to find out what's troubling him.

Your child can be upset for a number of reasons, even though these may seem trivial to you. For instance, not being able to draw well, being unable to climb the ladder up to the slide, or a comment from another child about his speed of running, could make your child feel unhappy. Talk to him when he seems down and try to offer a solution to his difficulty. Above all, reassure him that you think he is terrific.

Suitable Suggestions

By now he plays more cooperatively with his friends – they don't always share and take turns without arguing, but minor disagreements are becoming less frequent. His social skills are generally more mature. Make a special point of praising your child when he does play well with others, because this praise reinforces appropriate social behaviour. There's also no harm in reminding him, for example, before you take him for a visit to a friend's house that he

Right: At this age children begin to cooperate far more with each other during play and enjoy being part of shared games and activities.

Left: Somewhere around 3 years old children become more sensitive in their relationships with others and start to develop firmer friendships.

should behave properly and share toys and games with his friend.

Your child gradually becomes more amenable to your family rules and the frequency of challenges to the limits you set decreases. His thinking and language skills are more advanced, too, so now is a good time to spend more time explaining to him why you have rules. Don't make your discussion too long or complicated. Keep it basic. Once you have explained to him the reasons why, for instance, he shouldn't hit

Above: Your child will be far more confident in new situations and when you are not there.

someone, ask your child to explain the rule to you. As well as being a good way of testing his understanding, it also reinforces the message.

By this age your child is capable of undertaking basic tasks in the house, such as putting waste paper into the bin or putting his toys back in the cupboard. You may need to explain to him how to carry out such a task, but it will be within his capabilities and he will glow with pride when you then praise his helpfulness.

By now, his sense of self is more clearly defined. He is more aware of who he is, of his own distinctive strengths and weakness, of his likes and dislikes, and of the way other people react towards him as an individual. You'll find that he becomes indignant when he discovers that his personal space or possessions have been used by someone else. This is a very positive sign of his maturity, though you may find his pleas that things should be done his way rather tiresome! Involve him in minor decisions about clothes and food choices, where possible. Engage him in discussions about paint and wallpaper for his room when it's time to re-decorate.

Below: Your child will love exercising simple choices – like what ice cream to choose!

✦✦✦✦✦✦✦ Top · Tips ✦✦✦✦✦✦✦

1. Help him overcome any episodes of shyness. If he suddenly seems unwilling to attend his new playgroup or to go to a friend's house because of shyness, encourage him to go anyway. Tell him that there will plenty of exciting activities that he will miss if he doesn't go.

2. Model good social behaviour. One of the ways your child learns basic social skills is through imitation of you and others in your family at home. Let him see you cooperate and share with each other, without bickering.

3. Discourage aggressive behaviour. Some 3-year-olds go through a phase of slapping other children when they don't get their own way. Make sure yours understands that hitting anyone else is wrong – don't tolerate physical violence.

4. Buy him a small domestic pet to care for. Keeping a goldfish or hamster, for instance, is a good way to develop his concern for others, and is relatively trouble free. Suggest to your child that he should always feed the pet before he has his own meal and let him help with other aspects of its care.

5. Be there for him. As far as your child is concerned, every single thing that worries him is urgent – he isn't mature enough to wait for reassurance. Attend to his anxieties the moment you spot them, before they assume a greater importance in his mind.

Q How can I stop my child trying to do things that I know are much too difficult for him to achieve?

A He does this because he has such confidence in himself, and there is not much you can do to encourage him to be more realistic. However, when he does aim high and fails to reach his target, help him to avoid disappointment by reminding him of all his successes.

Q My 3-year-old loves watching adult television programmes. Could this be harmful to him?

A Psychological studies confirm that a child is influenced by the content of the programmes he watches, and there is no doubt that watching aggressive programmes can increase a child's aggressiveness. While many adult programmes have no harmful content, it is probably best to direct him towards those designed specifically for children.

Toys: child-sized furniture, soft ball, jigsaw puzzles, construction toys, dressing-up outfits, pedal toy, creative art materials

Index of Age Groups

General Index

Acknowledgements

Executive Editor – Jane McIntosh
Editor – Sharon Ashman
Executive Art Editor – Leigh Jones
Book Design – 2wo Design
Photography – Peter Pugh-Cook
Stylist – Aruna Mathur
Production Controller – Lucy Woodhead

The publisher would like to thank all the children and parents who took part in the photoshoot for this book for their time, energy, patience and cooperation. We would also like to thank the following organizations for allowing us to use their products:

The Corporation of London for allowing us to use the park at Highgate Wood, London

The Early Learning Centre, South Marston Park, Swindon, SN3 4TJ Tel: 01793 831300

Marks and Spencer Tel: 020 7268 3118

First published in Great Britain in 2001 by Hamlyn, a division of Octopus Publishing Group Limited, 2–4 Heron Quays, London E14 4JP

Copyright © Octopus Publishing Group Limited 2001
ISBN 0 600 60249 4

A catalogue record for this book is available from the British Library

Produced by Toppan Printing Company Ltd
Printed in China
10 9 8 7 6 5 4